You're A
Good Mom

(and your kids aren't so bad either)

PRAISE FOR
You're A Good Mom
(and your kids aren't so bad either)

"Jen Singer's hilarious, there's no doubt about it. Yet it's also refreshing to be reminded how great regular moms are. You'll nod and laugh all the way through."
—Sarah Smith, senior editor, *Parenting*

"Wow, what an easy, fun, enjoyable read! Jen's book provides welcome and sound advice to moms who just can't seem to stop the madness of trying to be perfect parents."
—Stefanie Wilder-Taylor, author of *Sippy Cups are Not for Chardonnay* and *Naptime is the New Happy Hour*

"As good as chocolate in book form! If this sanity-promising title caught your eye, you won't be disappointed: you'll find the exact same good-humored, feel-better wisdom on every page."
—Paula Spencer, author of *Momfidence! An Oreo Never Killed Anybody and Other Secrets of Happier Parenting* and *Woman's Day* "Momfidence" columnist

"Once again, Jen Singer gives moms a reality check—and an all-knowing giggle. Her writing is truly laugh-out-loud-funny! But it's also practical, with advice you can immediately act on. A welcome relief from other parenting books, especially since she admits that parenting isn't one-size-fits-all."
—Nicole Stagg, director, GoodHouseKeeping.com

"If you're a mom you need this laugh out loud look at motherhood. Jen Singer makes the ultimate sense and helps you find that elusive, happy medium in which children *and* moms thrive."
—Susan Newman, PhD, author of *Little Things Long Remembered: Making Your Children Feel Special Every Day*

You're A Good Mom

(and your kids aren't so bad either)

14 Secrets to Finding Happiness
Between Super Mom and Slacker Mom

JEN SINGER

SOURCEBOOKS, INC.®
NAPERVILLE, ILLINOIS

Published by Sourcebooks, Inc.
P.O. Box 4410, Naperville, Illinois 60567-4410
(630) 961-3900
Fax: (630) 961-2168
www.sourcebooks.com

Library of Congress Cataloging-in-Publication Data

Singer, Jen.
  You're a good mom (and your kids aren't so bad either) : 14 secrets to finding happiness between super mom and slacker mom / Jen Singer.
      p. cm.
  1. Motherhood—United States—Humor. 2. Mothers—United States—Humor.
I. Title.

HQ759.S556 2008
306.874'30973—dc22

                                        2007044255

          Printed and bound in the United States of America.
              VP 10 9 8 7 6 5 4 3 2 1

You're A Good Mom

(and your kids aren't so bad either)

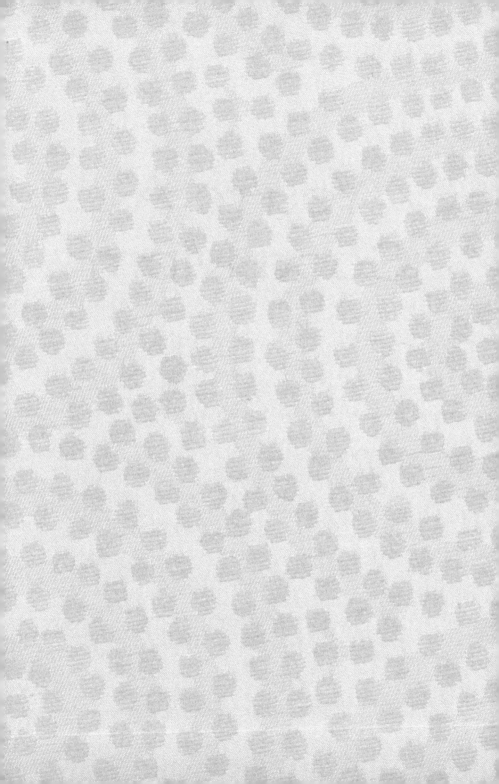

To Pete, a good dad and husband if there ever was one

CONTENTS

Introduction

When I was a kid, my mother and her sister had the same kind of "mom car," the precursor to the minivan: the 1975 Ford LTD Country Squire with fake-wood paneling. It was the kind of car that practically screamed, "Watch out! Station wagon full of untethered children on their way to the roller rink!"

Each morning my brother, my cousins, and I rode to school in my mother's burgundy Country Squire, and every afternoon we rode home in my Aunt Nancy's yellow wagon. But the rides couldn't have been more different.

In my mom's car, things were neat and orderly. You could find maps and guidebooks, arranged in alphabetical order, in her glove compartment. (You know, just in case you felt like taking an impromptu trip anywhere from the Lincoln Memorial to Fort Ticonderoga.) And her wagon's "way back" seat was unusually free of shin guards and school books, though after a long trip you might find my brother's collapsible magic wand and some foam balls.

In my aunt's car, on the other hand, various objects rolled around on every turn and flew forward at stoplights. There were toys and papers strewn about, and a half-open ashtray full of cigarette butts. When Aunt Nancy let my cousin Susan, then five, carry a banana split sundae into the car one summer evening, the rest of us kids dove into the way back. Sure enough, the gooey mess splattered onto the seat as soon as we pulled out of the Dairy Queen parking lot. And yet, Aunt Nancy seemed unfazed.

Both my mom and my aunt were thought of as perfectly fine mothers back in the day. My mom may have been considered "more involved" because she helped run the recreation department's Friday afternoon ice skating program, coached my soccer team, and served as class mom—for eleven years. But the other mothers never tried to keep up with her. They just let her run everything.

And nobody criticized my aunt, either, for her more laissez-faire approach to parenting. The neighbors didn't call Child Services, for example, when the police found my cousin Pete, then eight, shooting off (illegal) fireworks in his driveway. (My brother and I had ditched him as soon as we saw the squad car lights.)

In the end, my aunt's kids turned out just fine, and so did my mom's. Pete even managed to keep all of his fingers into adulthood.

But if my mother and her sister were moms of young kids today, facing the pressures of twenty-first-century perfect parenting and the likes of say, summer tutoring for students already earning straight A's, my mother would be branded a "Super Mom" and my aunt a "Slacker Mom." And their different styles of mothering would come under scrutiny by an entire society of know-it-alls.

Today, my mother would be the woman barking orders about the school fundraiser into her cell phone (she'd be co-chair, of course) while driving one kid to West African drumming class (for cultural well-roundedness combined with music lessons) and holding up algebra flash cards for her seven-year-old. (It's never too early to prep for the SATs, you know.)

Today, my aunt would be the woman who lets her tween go to school dressed in a Little Hottie top (belly shirt) and serves Cocoa

Puffs for dinner because why go to the supermarket again until she runs out of cigarettes? And yet she'd buy an $800 snowmaker on eBay (straight off the ski slopes!) to blow a mini-mountain in the backyard because, after all, it'd keep the kids out of her hair for a few hours.

Nowadays, it seems that you're either a Super Mom or a Slacker Mom, and there's little in between. But one's bad for Mom and the other can hurt the kids. What's a modern momma to do?

The parenting bar has been reset so incredibly high that today's moms struggle each day to keep up with all that they think is required to raise their kids right, from baby phonics tutoring to Tae Kwon Do for tots to ice hockey for children who have practically just learned how to walk.

And yet despite all this hyper-parenting, our generation has picked up quite a few slacker tendencies that aren't doing our kids any favors. Like getting parenting tips from *Access Hollywood*, as though celebrities with a gaggle of nannies, personal trainers, stylists, and publicists are good role models for real-world parenting. (Britney didn't drop the baby . . . or her drink.) Or ignoring the TV's parental controls and letting Junior watch a whack-'em-and-stack-'em episode of *The Sopranos*, because, hey, that scene was filmed at the ice cream shop right here in our downtown! How cool!

Lately, mommy books have encouraged twenty-first-century parents to cut themselves some slack, and I agree we should all just chill out a bit and let the kids play on their own. But it's not that simple. Our mothers' generation didn't have V-chips to block out the bad stuff on TV (we didn't need them—we had Donny & Marie on at 8 p.m., not *CSI: Crime Scene Investigators*), a magazine called *Baby Couture* featuring $42 Diesel T-shirts for toddlers, or YouTube, where kids can post all the stupid things they've ever done for all to see—including potential future employers. There are things in our brave new world that need more vigilance than our mothers ever even imagined, and Slacker Mom isn't cutting it.

We've become a generation of two-headed moms: One head remembers to pack the hand sanitizer and organic carrot sticks for the trip to the park, while the other lays out the "Lock Up Your Daughters" T-shirt for her son to wear and then cranks up the minivan sound system so the kiddies can enjoy the Black Eyed Peas' tribute to rear ends, "My Humps." ("What you gon' do with all that ass? All that ass inside them jeans?" I dunno, but I hope you leave it on your iPod, Mom.)

What's more, we're turning out a generation of children who are so accustomed to organized activities that they don't know how to entertain themselves, except, perhaps, to play videos that are too mature for them and surf the Internet unsupervised. So many of our kids are nervous about doing the *right* thing—by age ten—to get into the *right* college, they compete just to play on the best traveling soccer teams and take advanced classes so they can outscore their classmates on tests. And yet some of these very same kids are, uh, servicing each other on the middle-school bus ride home.

So, what's the secret to raising children these days? Mom from the middle. You can turn out perfectly good kids without playing keep-up with Super Mom or slipping into Slacker Mom's territory. It's just a matter of picking and choosing where to put your best efforts.

I've been using these parenting techniques ever since I had my own personal mom-tervention: The day I felt guilty for doing the laundry instead of spending time on the floor "bettering" my kids. I was a full-time, stay-at-home mom who spent upwards of one hundred hours a week with my kids, and yet folding my underpants made me feel like a bad mommy because I wasn't busy preparing my toddlers for Yale.

I wasn't alone in feeling the pressure to make every mothering moment count. In 2003, when I launched MommaSaid.net, my website for beleaguered moms, I discovered there were thousands of other mothers who, like me, were fed up with trying to follow the insane new rules of parenting. So I set out to make them—and me—feel better about how we're doing as mothers.

Most days, I blog about my life as the suburban mother of Nicholas and Christopher, two school-aged boys who talk to me through the bathroom door, and as the wife of Pete, an IT project manager who watches The Food Network like other men tune into ESPN. (The five most romantic words he's ever said to me are: "Get out of my kitchen." Oh, how I love him.)

I post photos of a bucket of worms my kids brought into the house and of my laundry piled up on my dryer taller than I am, so that other moms know they're not the only ones with homes that would make Martha Stewart gasp. And I give out awards—the Housewife Awards®—to offer a little recognition for the crazy and often funny things we endure as moms.

Most of all, I listen. Over the years, moms from around the world have told me they're tired. Tired of trying to keep up with the town alpha mom, who'll drive her Escalade right over you and your little bake sale if you don't do what she says. Tired of playing defense against the onslaught of naughty things the media expose our kids to right in our own homes. I understand, because I feel the same way.

Since my mom-tervention, I've relaxed a bit in some areas, such as letting my husband oversee Cub Scouts—"Daddy would love to take you camping while I stay home and watch chick flicks"—yet remain vigilant in others, like making the rule, "Just because it's a cartoon doesn't mean you can watch it." And so far, my kids are turning out fine. And so am I.

There's a safe spot somewhere in between the rule-the-town über moms and the donuts-for-dinner underachiever moms where you can be a good-enough mom and raise perfectly fine kids without losing your mind or your dignity. It's located somewhere between the Fort Ticonderoga map and the spilled banana split. And I'm here to help you find it.

15 Things You Won't Discover Until It's Too Late

1. If he gets really low like a Marine on a training course, your baby can fit completely under the couch.

2. Naptime ended fifteen minutes ago when your little one discovered how to get her rather full diaper off and put it on her favorite stuffed bear, giving a whole new meaning to "Winnie the Pooh."

3. There's no better hiding place for toy car wheels, Barbie heads, and half-eaten graham crackers than a tissue box, especially the one your husband's boss is reaching for right now.

4. Preschoolers can't play badminton, but they think they can. All you can do is pray for rain or a sudden acquisition of freakishly advanced athletic skills like the Williams sisters had, whichever comes first.

5. String beans fit nicely up a toddler's nose. French fries do, too, but it's less embarrassing to experience the vegetable disappearing act at McDonald's than at your mother-in-law's Thanksgiving dinner.

6. Your little one has the stomach flu, your pants are dry-clean-only and you're out of wipes.

7. The child lock on your car's windows is broken, as demonstrated by your preschooler, who just chucked the (ewwww!) asparagus from your grocery bags into the Burger King parking lot as you drove by it.

8. The power will be out for another seven hours, as will your flashlight, because the only working "C" batteries in the house are in the Sit n' Spin downstairs in the dark, scary basement, next to that creepy doll with the eyes that don't close.

9. The Tooth Fairy is out of small bills tonight.

10. The convoy of eleven school buses filled with rowdy kids that just drove past you is going to the same museum you're headed toward. And guess who else has to go potty.

11. The permanent markers are missing. And so are the pillows from your couch.

12. Your daughter's basketball registration was due this morning, the dog's shots were due ten days ago and whoops! So was your period.

13. You left a gallon of milk in the car three hours ago. But hey, at least you remembered to buy it this time, and that's a good start.

14. Hubby forgot to repack the diaper bag. Also, those rough, brown paper towels you find in mall bathrooms don't make good diapers. But the blouse you just bought for your job interview does.

15. Seven-year-olds sometimes don't hold your hand. Ten-year-olds rarely hug you, and teenagers pretty much just mumble, "Hi" — if you're lucky. Your little one, on the other hand, thinks you're better than the moon, Dora The Explorer, and Oreo cookies wrapped up in one.

Parts of this list originally appeared in *Parenting* magazine.

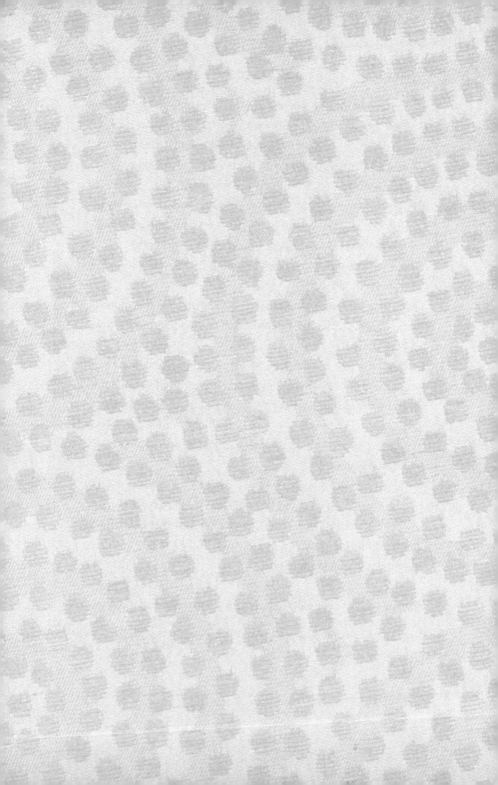

PART ONE

Don't Try to Keep Up with Super Mom.

She's addicted to hand sanitizer
and checking school rankings,
and she rarely sits down longer than it takes to pee.

SECRET ONE

Super Mom Is Faking It

You want to trip her as she glides by you at Back-to-School Night, looking like she just stepped off the cover of *Family Fun* magazine. In one hand, she holds a plate of homemade apple-shaped cookies. In the other, she has four hundred sign-up sheets for the school fundraiser, of which she is (naturally) the chair.

And then there's you, windblown, disheveled, and late (as usual), not to mention empty-handed because Hubby ate all your brownies last night. Once again, you're faced with the fact that this mom—a Super Mom, if there ever was one—has raised the mothering bar so impossibly high that your anxiety is skyrocketing along with it. No wonder you want to check her into the bake sale table like a hockey player during playoffs.

She is most definitely a Super Mom, and you're . . . what? Desperate to be like her. After all, she helped her son whittle a bar of Ivory soap into a museum-quality sculpture of Abraham Lincoln for a Cub Scouts project, while you let your son shave a few slices off his bar of soap and call it SpongeBob. Her son's project looks like it belongs in the Smithsonian with velvet ropes surrounding it. Your son's looks like an eight-year-old made it while watching the Mets game on TV, which is, of course, exactly what happened. If only, like her, you, too, had a Fine Arts degree. Then you wouldn't feel so inadequate when it comes time for you . . . er, your son . . . to do his school projects.

Able to Leap Tall Preschoolers in a Single Bound

You'd swear there's some sort of bat-signal that summons this woman at just the right moment, her hair glistening in the school gym lights, a cooler of chilled Gatorade bottles in multiple refreshing flavors at her feet as she trades inside jokes with the basketball coach, and then corners the principal for yet another pow-wow about her child's potential.

Meanwhile, you scrape the peanut butter off your sweatshirt and root through your purse for some lipstick, all the while mumbling under your breath, "Please don't sit next to me. Please don't sit next to me."

You don't want to hear about her latest project: her "craft room," an entire 16'×20' room dedicated to scrapbooking, sewing, needlepoint, and making homemade Halloween costumes that look like they belong on the cover of *Martha Stewart Kids*.

You, on the other hand, have nothing more than a "craft drawer," and that's only if you consider the following "crafty": plastic googly eyes, some kid-sized scissors that don't cut much of anything, and a dried-out glue stick covered in gold glitter. The last whimsical craft you tried to make—an egg-carton dragon— wound up in the toy box, crushed by a Tonka truck and stuck to Barbie's hair with a half-chewed gumdrop.

You long to be like Super Mom, because she seems to be what everyone thinks is a good mom these days—the kind of mom who puts her kids and their travel soccer games, piano lessons, Kumon tutoring, and elaborate dioramas of the White House made from sugar cubes before her own needs. The kind of mom who gives her kids the very best, so that one day she can put a Harvard sticker on the back window of her SUV and drive off to play bridge with the ladies at the club, where she'll brag about her children's scholarships, and, I dunno, the craft wing she'll add onto the house.

But do you want to pay $12,000 a year to send your four-year-old to a Chinese immersion school to "give her a leg up on her future?" Do you want to skip the swim team's trip to the water park so you can use the time to improve your kids' backstroke splits while everyone else is "wasting the day" in the wave pool? Do you want to be so busy running the town council, the home and school association, and the Mighty Mites hockey fundraiser that most nights you don't have time to eat dinner with your family? Will that make you happy? Better yet, will it really make you a better mother?

She's a Cross Between a Smooth Politician and a High-Profile Celebrity

But Super Mom isn't all that she appears to be. After all, it takes an enormous amount of energy to be the perfect mother—and even more energy to make it appear that way to everyone else.

In fact, here's a secret that Super Mom doesn't want you to know: She's really not perfect—just extremely adept at propaganda. She uses many of the same techniques that governments (for example, Hitler's Nazis) and Fortune 500 companies (like Enron) use to get their message out. You'll feel much better about how you measure up next to Super Mom when you realize it's all just smoke and mirrors.

To better prepare you to identify what's true and what's a load of bull, see the following chart. Super Mom's statements are matched with the type of propaganda they represent:

The Super Mom Propaganda Machine

Propaganda	Statement
Appealing to Authority Appeals to a person in authority to support an idea or situation	"Please tell the principal that I would love to help the school by creating a taskforce to identify which lunch items are not healthy for our children."
Appealing to Fear Making a big deal out of a small problem	"Well, certainly you're concerned about the safety of your children...that's why we need to ban all games of tag and other contact sports at recess!"
Argumentum ad Nauseam Tireless repetition until it's taken as truth	"We cut our vacation short so Jimmy could be here for the game today. The team can't play without their star pitcher! And we hired him a personal trainer, because that's what college scouts want to see. Oh! Did I mention he holds the no-hitter record for the entire county? Look at that! Nobody's got a curveball like our Jimmy."
Bandwagon Approach Persuading people to take the action that "everyone else" is taking	"I'm sure you've heard that the women's club, the recreation department, and the class moms have all gotten behind the

	referendum to build a state-of-the-art Astroturf football field. After all, don't you want the best for our town's children?"
Glittering Generalities Emotionally appealing words with no concrete back-up	"We all know that the children who grow up to be the most successful adults have been exposed to a wide variety of activities and opportunities. That's why my Madeleine is taking ballet, flute, swim lessons, karate, and voice lessons."
Scapegoating Blaming someone who isn't actually responsible	"I'd be class mom again this year if the selection committee wasn't so intimidated by my creativity. I guess that if they don't want the second graders to learn about our founding fathers from the twenty-three paper maché George Washington heads I made for the President's Day celebration, I can't do anything about it."
Stereotyping Arousing prejudices by labeling	"Well, my son would be the valedictorian if that Asian family hadn't moved into town. You know how it is with them: They're so naturally smart and ambitious. We just can't compete."

She's an Even Better Spin Doctor Than the White House Spokesperson

To Super Mom, appearances are everything. That's why she wears full makeup and a fashionable outfit (Marc Jacobs, of course) to pick up her antibiotics at the pharmacy, even though her sinus infection makes her head feel like a melon in the baggage compartment of a jumbo jet at 30,000 feet.

She says she puts her home on the town's annual house tour to help raise money for the local hospital, but really she just wants to show off her built-in cappuccino machine and her $8,000 plasma TV. The house tour is her own personal version of MTV's *Cribs*, the show that tours celebrities' homes in all their glory. And thanks to her very own meditation room, complete with a life-sized gold Buddha statue and indoor waterfall, she's the Snoop Dogg of the neighborhood. At least, that's what she wants you to think.

Lucky for her, there are no paparazzi following her around to snap pictures of her lugging the garbage to the end of the driveway in the pouring rain or screaming at her kids for leaving filthy footprints on her white carpets. And there are no journalists digging up her dirt, including her four months in rehab for her pain pill addiction, or her husband's affair with his boss. These are the things you'll never find out about her—just the way she likes it.

Still, She Gets Your Goat

Yet you just can't help yourself, can you? You keep comparing yourself to Super Mom and her impossibly clean SUV (where are the Goldfish cracker crumbs and cleat-shaped mud?) with the "My child is an honor student" bumper sticker. She's the popular girl from tenth grade all grown up, raising her own popular kids who look like they belong in a Cheetah Girls video . . . if the

Cheetah Girls had a song about Ivy League-bound kids and their spelling bee championship trophies.

You can't stop measuring yourself against her and her size-four pants, PTA presidency, and a new $60,000 H-2. But if you don't, you're going to make yourself miserable trying to keep up with appearances.

Jen's Tips for Overcoming Super Mom Envy
Stick to What You Know

If your neighbor can make crafts out of tissue boxes and pipe cleaners (which she always has on hand in her craft room) but you can barely glue together two Popsicle sticks, don't try to compete with her. You will only set yourself up for failure—and the worst kind of failure: the public, everyone-in-the-town-saw-it kind of failure.

For example, if you're craft-challenged like me, your homemade Halloween costumes will fall terribly short of their mark. Take the year I decided, "I can make a ghost costume!" I cut and sewed some white fabric, even creating a removable mask that could be pushed back like a hood so my son could take it off to see where he was walking.

But when he rounded the corner of the street during his school's annual Halloween parade, my stomach jumped—he didn't look like a ghost at all. My neighbor Kim asked, "Uh, what's Chris supposed to be?" I replied, "He's supposed to be a ghost, but I suppose he looks like he's heading to a Klan meeting, right?" Yep: I sent my child to school in a homemade outfit tailor-made for a white supremacists' rally.

So when my other son decided one Halloween that he wanted to be a ghost, I rushed out to Party City to buy a $17 Cool Ghoul costume with plastic chains and a plastic mask. It didn't win him any originality prizes at the Cub Scouts Halloween party, but it didn't leave other parents wondering if we were holding secret KKK meetings in the woods behind our house, either.

Every town has a mom (or two or three) who can create ridiculously ornate, professional-looking crafts and baked goods. She's the mom who offers to bring the dessert for International Day in the first grade and ends up hand-painting the flags of twenty-four countries in icing on the cupcakes. (She even gets the Arabic on the Saudi flag right.) Imagine the Jell-O dessert recipe you copied from an ad in *Woman's Day* sitting next to the cupcakes. I say, why bother?

Let the Town Crafter do her thing while you concentrate on whatever *you're* good at doing. I'm adept at making small children burst into giggles. So while my Town Crafter is busy helping children glue together their picture frames at the December holiday party, I read them a silly story, complete with voices and sound effects. When the teacher's not looking, I throw in a burp. This is what I'm good at, and though it'll never earn me heaps of praise at the school bake sale, I will remain a celebrity among the elementary school children in my town. She may be our town's Martha Stewart, but I'm Elvis.

Better yet, I did not have to bake anything, cut anything, measure anything, glue anything, or frost anything. I did not have to call my neighbors to beg for eggs after I ruined my first batch of cookies, or frantically call my sister-in-law for late-night instructions on how to ice cakes using a pastry bag.

I stick to what I know, and so far I feel far less stressed than I used to. Do my kids care that I sent them in with store-bought cookies for their birthday treats? Nope, not since the year I made baseball-bat-with-ball cookies that turned out looking like little yellow penises.

Did You Know?

Super Mom . . .

. . . sleeps sitting up in a chair surrounded by her scrapbooking supplies and the seating chart for her husband's surprise fortieth birthday party (for three hundred of their closest friends)?

. . . repels mud just like Wonder Woman wards off bullets with her bracelets?

. . . keeps math flash cards in her glove compartment, and can recite all the names of U.S. presidents — in order?

. . . had lip-liner tattooed on to save her time in the morning for more important things, like grilling the kids on the U.S. presidents?

. . . never, ever drinks more than one glass of wine, because she says "Loose lips sink ships"?

. . . alphabetizes her spices, color codes her closets, and charts her workouts?

. . . is frequently the number one topic of gossip in the teacher's lunchroom, where she's known as "Princess Pushy"?

. . . irons bedsheets and scrubs grout with a toothbrush every Tuesday?

. . . finds time to put her feet up only at the gynecologist's office?

Let Her Win

Super Mom is gloating because she has won the praise of the school principal and most of the teachers for the mural she painted on the cafeteria wall. Congratulate her and move on, content in the fact that you've had more sleep and cleaner clothes than she's had all month. Think of her as being in a different category than you're in. Not better. Just different.

It's a bit like college: She's dual majoring in Art and Early Childhood Education with night classes in an Accelerated Executive Program, while you're majoring in Psychology with a minor in Sports Management.

That's why she spends her weekends hand-painting holiday cards for every teacher, the superintendent, and the school bus driver, while you're busy trying to figure out how come your kid is dribbling the ball the wrong way down the soccer field.

So, if she beats you to the sign-up sheet for the kindergarten's Thanksgiving party, let it go. Rather, you should thank her, because she has just freed up your Saturday to take the kids to the movies, or to teach your child which way to dribble the ball on the soccer field. Super Mom has given you and your children the gift of time.

So what if the teachers surround her, ooohing and aaaahing, as she unveils the most amazing 3-D pilgrim cakes, while you trace the children's hands to make what she calls a "classic" (read: unimaginative) turkey craft? She spent her last few days and nights carving desserts shaped like our country's forefathers. You spent yours reading to your kids.

Remember, your kids are the ones who'll decide if you'll go into a nursing home or live with them someday, not the teachers or the principal or your neighbor or the owner of the craft shop who knows Super Mom by name.

Sign Her Up

Delegate some of your volunteering duties to Super Mom, and you won't have to make several hundred photocopies or stencil any posters for weeks—maybe the entire school year.

If you've made the bold move of taking charge of an event, such as the annual community egg hunt, or even if you've just stumbled into it, take heart. With Super Mom on your committee, you won't have to do all the grunt work. She'll do it for you.

She's used to being in charge, and she'll do all she can to make sure that she usurps your power. But don't let her steamroll you to the point that you wind up sitting in the corner, peeling a few dozen price tags and sticking them on baked goods while she runs the show. Rather, pick a big job that keeps her busy and out of your hair while simultaneously removing a sizable responsibility from your plate, such as overseeing the catering or running the admissions booth.

But what if you're in charge and someone else—who hasn't even signed up to help—decides to butt in? Oh, I've been blindsided by these moms. They pretend to be helpful by giving me "tips" on coaching my soccer team, and then plant themselves in the middle of our practice, barking orders at the kids. When I ask why they didn't sign up to coach, they say, "Oh, I don't have the time."

Here's what I do: I ask them to stand behind the goal and retrieve soccer balls. When they're bored with that (or when they've been pegged in the head one too many times) I say, "You know what would be a big help to the team? Could you oversee a sign-up sheet for parents to bring snacks and water to the games?"

As long as these moms have something to be in charge of, they'll back off. And then you can get back to coaching, organizing, planning, or whatever you need to do.

Cheat

She's got not one, but *three* Christmas trees up and decorated in her house—and it's not even December yet. She's even got a menorah in case she entertains during Hanukkah, and a book about Kwanzaa on her coffee table. She's got it all covered. Or so it seems.

It takes an enormous amount of time and effort to keep up the kind of appearances that Super Mom does. Assuming she doesn't have a staff to help her, she's the one who's lugging her elaborate mum-and-pumpkin display from the farm stand and setting it up on her front lawn.

She's gotta be tired.

You can make yourself look more put-together by taking some shortcuts. Shhh! No one has to know. Here's how.

Spend extra for back-ups. Ever since I pulled a pair of stinky, filthy soccer socks out of the hamper to put on one of my kids (well, okay, I did it twice), I started buying multiple pairs of soccer socks at the beginning of the season, thereby increasing my chances of finding a clean pair on game day.

I do the same thing not only with sports supplies, such as shin guards, but also with mittens, hats, regular socks (I swear our clothes dryer eats them), Cub Scouts slides (those metal neckerchief holders they lose behind the bleachers at every pack meeting), jackets, and anything else I've found myself rushing around to find before school, a game, or an activity. That way, my kid isn't the one with the frozen red hands at recess, and I look like a fabulous mother.

Get an electronic organizer. If you're not fortunate enough to have a job that doles out BlackBerries to its employees, invest in a Palm Pilot or other electronic organizer than can download to your computer's calendar, thereby doubling your chances of remembering when the Girl Scouts camping trip will be held.

The best feature of an electronic organizer is that you can easily keep several people's schedules at once, so when one kid has lacrosse practice at the same time another kid has debate club, you can mark it without filling the day's entire box, as on a printed calendar.

Befriend the organized. Every group has one: the mom who always seems to know what's going on. She's the mom you call when you aren't sure what time Back-to-School Night starts or when the permission slips for the fourth-grade class trip are due. Seek out that mom in each activity your kids participate in, and you'll never lose track of where they have to be and when.

Could You Be a Super Mom?

If you've ever studied for the SATs (or tutored your kids for the test), you'll be familiar with the format of this quiz.

Comprehension

Read the sample passage and answer the accompanying question.

Emily has a geography project due on Thursday, but she doesn't have the supplies for the accompanying diorama. Her mother stops at the craft store between flute lessons and basketball practice and buys miniature plastic trees, seventeen different colored paints, a bag of beads, and glue gun refills.

That night, Mom works on the diorama while searching the Internet for the history of the Philippines. Emily is busy at the dress rehearsal for a play she's starring in this weekend.

In this passage, we learned that . . .
   a. Like a shark, Emily's mom doesn't sleep. Rather, she quietly treads while keeping a watchful eye on her prey.
   b. Emily's mom has a huge craft supply store bill.
   c. Emily has way the hell too much stuff to do.
   d. All of the above

Sentence Completion

Choose the fragment that best completes this sentence.

A good mother . . .

. . . knows where to buy the best tap shoes, junior hockey equipment, and favors (i.e. her carpenter "assisted" her son in creating his Cub Scouts Pinewood Derby race car, which won first place this year).

. . . hires a personal soccer trainer for her second grader.

. . . programs her BlackBerry to remind her to drill her children on their spelling words each day at 4:30 p.m.

. . . has her very own personal shopper to assist her at The Children's Place, Kids Foot Locker, and Learning Express.

. . . packs a note that says "I love you" in her kids' lunchboxes every now and then.

Vocabulary

Each question below consists of a related pair of words. Select the pair that best matches the sample pair.

TUTOR: SATURDAYS
LEG UP: SACRIFICE
IMPRESS: COLLEGE ADMISSION OFFICERS
SO LONG RETIREMENT FUND: HELLO ANXIETY ATTACKS
SORRY, KIDS: JIMMY CAN'T PLAY OUTSIDE BECAUSE HE'S GOT TO DO HIS CALCULUS DRILLS TODAY

Algebra

Read this passage and then answer the question.

Today, Brandon's mother managed to get soccer banned at recess (too dangerous and stains her son's new khakis), drove 17 miles to persuade the swim team coach to choose her third grader over her sister's kid (while promising to fund two dozen new team sweatshirts), and made 138 miniature ghosts for her annual Halloween window display.

How many people did Brandon's Mother piss off today?
   a. The kids at recess, the swim coach, and her next-door neighbor, who suddenly wondered if her two jack-o'-lanterns and her "Trick or Treat" sign were adequate.
   b. Her first grader, her sister, and her husband, who said, "Please tell me you didn't pin all those damn ghosts to the new window frames."
   c. The head of the swim team's annual fundraiser for team clothing and half the teachers in the school, who have to calm down numerous soccer-loving kids who didn't have a chance to blow off steam at recess.
   d. All of the above

Geometry
Read this passage and then answer the question:

If a group of mothers is jockeying for the best view of their children at the dance recital, who will get closest to the stage?

   a. The mom who has volunteered to shoot video for a post-recital exposé entitled, *Shall We Dance? Preparing America's Future Rockettes.*
   b. The mom who sewed eighteen Vegas showgirl costumes in sizes 2T and 3T for the recital.
   c. The mom who had enough connections to get Michael Flatley from *Lord of the Dance* to choreograph tonight's show.
   d. All of the above

SECRET TWO

You're Too Big to Sit at the Tea Party Table

You finally sit down with the newspaper and the reheated mug of coffee you left in the microwave four hours ago. Out of the corner of your eye, you spot your preschooler trying to play Candy Land by herself. Suddenly, a wave of guilt overcomes you like a sea of tweens rushing the stage at *High School Musical: The Concert*. You just can't stop it.

You put down the *New York Times* (which, frankly, has been nothing more than a very expensive weather report and calendar since you became a mother) and sit down next to the game board for even more floor time with your daughter. After all, you're supposed to spend quality, one-on-one time with your kids, building their brains and enriching their lives. At least, that's what the parenting experts say.

Your mother, on the other hand, thinks you spend too much time with the kids. She never wasted her mornings trying to make puppets out of lunch bags with you, so why should you go and play with Elmer's glue and mini pom-poms now? She'd much rather you get your laundry done, especially since it's been piled up on the clothes dryer all week—and the pile is now taller than you are.

You point out to your mother that (a) so what if the only time she ever used a glue gun was to stick the grip back on her tennis racket? And (b) she used to shoo you outside the house to play all day back when, apparently, there were no pedophiles lurking in the bushes. Things are different now, you tell her. Motherhood is different now.

We Focus Entirely Too Much on Our Kids

You're right, moms these days spend more time with their children than our mothers' generation did. According to a University of Maryland study, today's mothers spend an average of 12.9 hours a week on childcare activities, up from 10.6 hours in 1965. And yet, we still think that's *not enough*, probably because we think we're supposed to cram into those 13 hours things our mothers never even dreamed of doing, like playing Mozart for our babies when they're still in utero.

My aunt certainly didn't seem to worry whether she was spending enough time with her children. Even when my cousin didn't learn to walk until he was eighteen months old, she didn't seem alarmed. He eventually got around to it, and he's been walking ever since. (Well, except in college, when as social chairman of his fraternity he likely went back to crawling, at least on weekends.) My aunt didn't fret, and my cousin eventually caught up.

But when my son came home with a less-than-stellar report from his preschool gym class, I panicked. His teacher suggested that his gross motor skills weren't up to par, and advised me to take him for physical therapy testing and, "while you're at it," occupational testing for his fine motor skills because he held his pencil "funny" in his classroom.

So after a few sleepless nights and some arguments with my insurance company about coverage, I dragged my four-year-old to test what only twenty-first-century neurotic parents could be concerned about: whether or not the boy could skip. You know, because every corporate executive ought to know how to *skip* into a conference before filling out his "My Name Is" badge and grabbing a danish. This is, indeed, a skill for life. At least, that's what his preschool gym teacher had scared into me.

Testing Gross Motor Skills, Testing Mom's Patience

An experienced physical therapist—who clearly was more accustomed to working with children who had *real* physical problems— spent twenty minutes assessing my preschooler while he jumped over foam blocks, walked up and down a small flight of stairs, and, yes, skipped. He was no Little Red Riding Hood, but he could do something that sort of resembled skipping without tripping himself up. Meanwhile, I held my breath.

"I'm not used to working with such a high-functioning child," the PT exclaimed while checking off all the "normal range" boxes on my son's evaluation sheet.

After we finished the jumping and skipping tests, an occupational therapist said pretty much the same thing, suggesting that I work with my son on his pencil grip over the summer. "If it doesn't improve, you can always come back in the fall when he's in kindergarten," she said in the same tone one might use with a grown-up who likes to wear Hello Kitty socks to Back-to-School Night.

I began to wish I could disappear into my beanbag chair with my "high-functioning child" and my insurance co-pay. Why were we wasting an afternoon and our family's annual insurance deductible getting my son evaluated? Oh yeah, because the teacher frightened me. And because I'd heard other parents say things like, "My nephew wasn't tested and now he has physical therapy three times a week." I mean, what if my son never met that important milestone of skipping?

Uh, I dunno. Is there a skipping requirement on Harvard's admissions application? I doubt it.

The same kid who could barely skip back in preschool is now a year-round athlete who can dribble a basketball with either hand and do cannonballs off the dock at our community lake, all while simultaneously humming the theme song to *Star Wars*. So far, he hasn't skipped around the bases after a home run, but I imagine he could if he wanted to. He is a "high-functioning child," after all.

And so, I wonder: Do we focus too much on our kids because we're made to feel useless if we don't? We certainly agonize over missed milestones and even signs of genius in a way that never concerned our mothers. After all, there was no kindergarten readiness testing thirty years ago. Back then it went like this:

"Are you five?"

"Yes."

"Then you're ready for kindergarten."

Not us. We lose sleep over the indicator or sign we might miss, thereby allowing our kid to fall behind everyone else's kid. And we can't have that. Not in a world where parents hire coaches to help their kids write their college application essays. We pay a lot of attention to every detail of our kids' lives—too much attention—and we're burning ourselves out in the process. It makes me wonder what we're doing to our kids.

Definitions: What Modern-Day Parenting Lingo Would Have Meant to Our Mothers

Floor time: Time spent waxing the kitchen floor while the kids amuse themselves in the playpen

Time out: A short break during a sporting event; taking a break from laundry to watch *Days of Our Lives*

Make good choices: *The Carol Burnett Show* instead of *Hee Haw*

Tummy time: Tending to an upset stomach after too many gin and tonics at last night's cocktail party down the street

Kindergarten readiness: Your kid's fifth birthday

Use your words: "Knock it off, kids!"

Quality time: Reading the newspaper in the car outside the movie theater where the kids are watching *The Bad News Bears*

Teachable moments: School

Always On Call

I felt like I was on stage, performing for an audience that had fallen asleep in their drinks. I was pushing my son, then four months old, in his stroller, while pointing out the scenery. "See the birdie, Nicholas?" I asked. "And there's a deer!" I whispered. "And that? That's a Porsche Boxster with 2.5-liter dual-overhead-cam and six-cylinder-produced 201 horsepower."

I was so tired from caring for a colicky baby that I was downright punchy, but dammit, I was going to better my baby anyhow. I had read in a parenting book that I was supposed to keep a running dialogue going so my newborn would learn my voice, language, and, I suppose, what kind of cars our neighbors drive.

Frankly, I thought the whole thing was silly: He couldn't understand what I was saying, nor could he see past his elbows, so why put in that kind of effort when I was so sleep-deprived that the stroller started to push *me* back down the hill near my house, even though the wind was blowing in my favor?

But I feared he'd fall behind in his development if I didn't point things out to him. After all, that's what the books said to do.

And so I rambled on about landscaping equipment, drainage pipes, and small woodland animals. Oh, and really nice sports cars, too, but that was just to keep me from letting the air out of the tires. "See the woman in the souped-up convertible, Nicholas? She has no idea what it's like to wake up every ninety minutes for four months straight. Not like Mommy does."

And that's where it started: being on call for my kids *all of the time.* Well, perhaps it started even earlier, at the pediatrician's office on the day we got the dreaded diagnosis of colic. Nicholas had been crying upwards of six hours a day, and I had been holding him while pat-pat-patting his back for those six hours a day.

So when I placed him on the examining table for the doctor to examine him, I figured she had it under control. But no. He started crying, and she gestured to me to help soothe him. "Shhhh!" she whispered while looking over her shoulder at me. In other words, "Mommy, this is your job. Get to it."

I wanted to shout, "Holy crap, lady. Can't you do it? You're a doctor! I've been doing that every day for about as long as you spend in the office. I really don't need the practice, thank you." But I was guilted into rushing to his side once again.

"See the lazy doctor, Nicholas? She can't let Mommy zone out for a few desperately needed minutes before she gives me the diagnosis of the terrible C-word and assures me it'll last only three months."

And I couldn't forget about the Zero to Three Initiative, a nonprofit organization designed to teach parents how to make the best of their babies' and toddlers' lives, which asserted that young children's brains are more open to "learning and enriching influences" than at any other time in their lives. The initiative was aimed at less educated parents who might not have learned to nurture their children as they should. But somehow, middle- and upper-class mothers got a hold of the information, and suddenly there was Baby Einstein, baby sign language, and other modern parenting tools. Certainly women like my mother-in-law, who had raised three kids who entertained themselves in the playpen, find such modern parenting must-haves just plain stupid.

We took the Zero to Three Initiative so seriously, we thought we had to make the best of every single moment of our children's formative years. And the right way to make the best of every moment was to be available at all times, like Paula Abdul's personal assistant.

And then we have safety concerns our mothers didn't. Our kids can't just go out and play down the street all day like we did. Rather, we've got to know where our kids are at all times. All this constant monitoring of our kids has helped create one neurotic generation of parents who have a very hard time letting go. And yet, we really need to. We really don't need to always be on call for our kids.

Jen's Tips for Teaching Your Kids to Entertain Themselves
If They Say, "I Do It," Let Them

If your toddler insists, "I do it," just let him, assuming, of course, that safety isn't an issue and you're not rushing to catch a ferry or something. If he wants to try to put on his shoe, don't tell him, "Now Ethan. That shoe belongs on the other foot. Let Mommy do that for you."

Because the more that you, the Mommy, do things for Ethan, the more you set yourself to become his personal assistant, so that by the time he's ten, he'll expect you to cut up his meat every night and pack up his homework each morning.

Then, when he's a teen, you'll be rushing the hockey equipment he forgot to bring with him to 6 a.m. practice (again) and filling out his college applications. God help him when he's finally on his own. He won't know what to do.

Sure, you'll spend some agonizing moments trying to leave the playground while your son attempts to put away the Cheerios all by himself. But while you're anxiously watching him stuff the half-open baggie upside-down into the diaper bag, think of it as a deposit into your Mom Sanity Account for down the road.

A year or so from now, while all the other moms are packing up their gear like sherpas headed for Kilimanjaro while their kids run amok, your preschooler will automatically help you get ready to leave. And you'll look like Mother of the Year. "I do it" is like buying bonds: costly now, but it pays off later on.

Stop Stalking the School

If your child knows you're standing in the hallway, peering around her classroom's door, it'll take her much longer to get used to being on her own. Your presence tells her, "You shouldn't feel safe here." And it tells the teacher, "I'm a neurotic mother who can't just let go already and head off to Target or the computer like everybody else."

Perhaps you're thinking, "But you don't understand. My Ellie is very shy." So then, you're going to stick around the classroom to give her something to cling to in case some kid looks at her funny? Exactly how is that teaching her to be independent?

Consider this: Chances are, her preschool teacher has dealt with shy children before, not to mention the kid who doesn't know the meaning of "indoor voice," the I-don't-know-how-to-share-so-I'm-going-to-clock-anyone-who-comes-near-me kid, the sorta kinda potty-trained child, the only-plays-with-his-best-buddy kid, and the child who hides in the corner talking to stuffed animals until snack time.

Your Ellie is in good hands. After all, you did all the research, interviews, and flow chart comparisons that led you to choose her school, didn't you? Of course you did, or else you wouldn't be in the hallway, pretending to examine the artwork on the bulletin board. You care way too much not to.

Please take this advice from a serial class mom: You *can* spend too much time at your kid's school. Signing up to bring in cupcakes (or, in these health-conscious times, oatmeal raisin cookies, no icing, no nuts) for the Valentine's Day party is one thing. Serving as a lunch aide *every single day* and becoming as much a fixture in the school copy room as the laminating machine is quite another.

There's a line between being an involved mother and a stalker, and it's in your child's best interest if you don't cross it, no matter how tempting it is. I nearly crossed that line when my younger son was in kindergarten, and the teacher asked me to stop in once a week to help the children write stories on the computer.

When I entered the classroom to the kind of excited gasps and enthusiastic waving (accompanied by shouts of "Hi, Mrs. Singer!") that one might see on the red carpet at the Oscars, I felt like a rock star. And I rather enjoyed hearing the stories that only five-year-olds can write, like the one about the number two: "Two follows one. Two comes before three. I like the number two. The end." If only lawyers could write in such a pithy manner.

It was tempting to take my Very Important Mom status too far. I could have suggested how the teacher could better use her Circle Time. I could have hung out by the principal's office so I could discuss the school lunch menu. Worse, I could have looked over my son's shoulder and advised him to move his blocks a little farther from Daniel's in case they fall into each other.

I was heady with influence—something that other mothers seemed to envy. I watched some moms deliver flowers to the secretaries in the front office or "leave a little something" (aka home-made cinnamon bread) in the teachers' room and I thought, *Well, I should do that, too, so that my kids get the attention they deserve.* I had the access. I had the power.

Instead, I chose to spend my hour simply helping kids write, because that's what I was asked to do, and then I quietly exited the building. Anything more would have been stalking.

You're Not Your Child's Entertainment Director

I am the hostess of the frat house for fourth graders. On many afternoons, you will find a half-dozen boys—most of them not mine—racing through my yard (and my pantry), playing all sorts of games, some made-up—like the one involving a fort in the woods and hockey sticks as guns—and some standard, like soccer. But please note: I am not their entertainment director.

If the boys can't come up with something to do with a garage full of sporting goods and various games, they know they'll be sent home.

But it wasn't always that way.

My sons used to play with two boys down the street. Or, I should say, my sons played with the kids' toys, and I played with the four-year-old who couldn't wait for Mrs. Singer to come over, because she shot baskets with him and taught him how to lift a hockey puck into the net.

I stopped being my kids' entertainment director after I spent an afternoon covered in gray paint, making a toy castle out of an empty Amazon box, toothpicks, and a black Sharpie pen. By the time "we" were done, the boys had lost interest, choosing instead to watch the castles on *Dragon Tales* while I put Band-Aids on my fingers from all that slicing of cardboard (and skin).

"It's done!" I announced.

"What are we doing next?" my son asked, his hand in a bag of Goldfish crackers and one eye on the TV.

I realized then that I was putting in way more hours than most parents, and though I was filling it with fun stuff to do, it was too much. My sons didn't know how to entertain themselves. And why should they? They had their own personal concierge, who constantly came up with FUN-FUN-FUN stuff to do, from making race tracks on the kitchen floor with masking tape to digging up worms with a plastic beach shovel for "worm races." (Trust me: You don't want to know.)

From the outside, I'm sure I looked like a cast-off from *Captain Kangaroo,* seemingly making the most of the precious time I had with my children. But as a full-time stay-at-home mom, I had upwards of one hundred hours a week of precious time with my kids, and they weren't learning how to entertain themselves because of it. Our mothers didn't micromanage our play like that. Of course, our play took place in the woods or the yard while our mothers had no idea where we were for hours at a time. So I'm not sure that's a great comparison for twenty-first-century parenting.

Still, they certainly didn't read such overkill as one article I found on the Internet called "How to Help Your Child Get the Most Out of Playtime." They didn't fuss over such things as the article's directives to "encourage imaginative play" or "build self-esteem by playing alongside your child" like we do. And they didn't introduce games for us to play at playdates, and then "unobtrusively supervise" the activity, as the article suggests. They just assumed we knew how to play. That's what kids do, right?

I am all for acting like a kid. After all, I'm a ten-year-old boy trapped in a housewife's body. But when a little fun crosses the line into something akin to organizing the Summer Olympics, you need to step back and let the kids play.

Even when your kids are as young as babies, let them hang out on their own for a while every day. Otherwise, they learn, "If I pick up the little stuffed bunny and shove its face into my mouth, Mommy will appear!" like my kids did. Toddlers will come to understand, "If I play with my Learn & Groove™ Counting Maracas, Mommy will rush over to say numbers with me." Preschoolers will figure out how to get you to put down the phone and entertain them, and older kids will whine, "I'm booooooored" to persuade you to drop everything and plan their afternoons like a volunteer at the Chamber of Commerce in Lancaster, Pennsylvania.

Here's a twenty-first-century word to remember: *Empower* your kids to entertain themselves. Someday, when they find themselves working the Thursday-night late shift at Dairy Queen on a cold, rainy night, they will thank you.

Finally, stop micromanaging playdates and let your kids enjoy their friends. And then you can enjoy the coffee you left in the microwave hours ago.

Crimes Against Mom Police Report

Crime Information

☒ **Petty Theft** (i.e. anything easily replaced at Target)

☐ **Grand Theft** (i.e. pricey wedding gifts you've hidden in your dining room, aka "The No-No Room")

☐ **Lost Property** (i.e. the Tupperware lids you haven't seen since your child discovered they fly "like UFOs, Mommy!")

☐ **Suspicious Circumstances** (Certainly, the dog couldn't have put on your new gauchos all by himself.)

☐ **Theft from Unlocked Vehicle** (Hmmm. Someone keeps calling from your cell phone to shout, "Swiper, no swiping!" and hangs up.)

Type of Vandalism: ☐ Graffiti (crayon) ☐ Graffiti (lipstick) ☐ Graffiti (GASP! permanent marker)

☐ **Toilet paper** (stuffed in toilet in large quantities with Barbie's shoes and a dozen animal crackers)

Location where crime occurred:

Right behind my back, as usual.

When did this incident occur?

While I was making dinner, the kids were (supposedly) watching TV in the other room, and my husband was driving home in his pristine car, probably listening to NPR or other thoughtful grown-ups who use words with multiple syllables.

Suspect Description

Clothing Description	Gender	Age	Height	Hair	Additional Information
Pink pants with embroidered flowers and a matching shirt that reads, "Girls Rule, Boys Drool."	Female	twenty-two months (going on thirty years)	three feet two inches	two pigtails: one missing a pink bow and the other held together with chewing gum	May be armed with a half-full sippy cup and one very strong arm. Approach with caution— and perhaps a lollipop.

Crime Narrative

The suspect entered the kitchen way more quietly than she had ever been at storytime in the library, that's for sure. I was busy making chicken nuggets, so I didn't see or hear her climb up on the kitchen chair, reach for my purse, and pull out my wallet.

It wasn't until I heard a plunking noise coming from the heating duct that I realized that the contents of my wallet had been dropped to a fiery death. My credit cards, my driver's license, my insurance cards, and worst of all, my Starbucks Frequent Visitor Card, were all wedged deep into the bowels of our heating system. The only thing that survived was a photo of my daughter, dressed like an angel for Halloween. My library card—and my patience—were not so lucky.

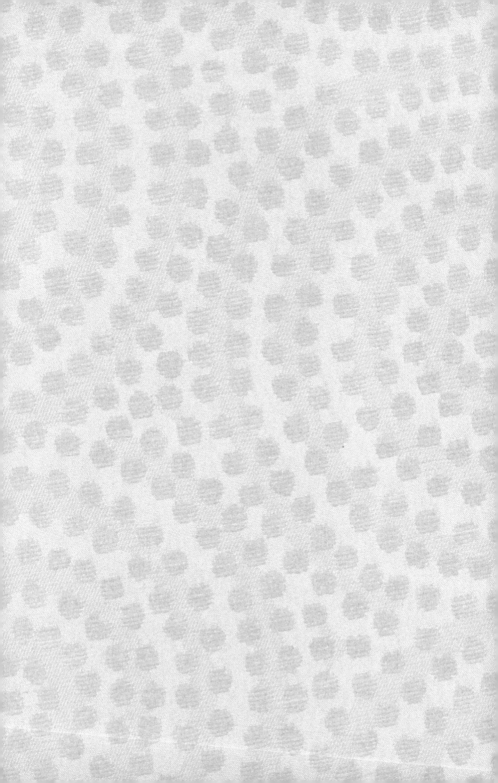

SECRET THREE

Don't Answer the Phone When the Class Mom Calls

I shouldn't have answered the phone.

One of the security guards from our lake community was ticked off. "Mrs. Singer!" he barked. "There's a bunch of moms at the lake wondering when the movie's gonna start, but the screen's not even up."

I wasn't in charge of the Movie Night put on by the Mother's Group, but somehow, a couple of neighbors thought I was, even though I hadn't served on the Mother's Group board in at least two years. Even though when I was on the board, I was not the president. And yet when there was a problem with a Mother's Group activity, someone would inevitably call Mrs. Singer. Now and then, they still do.

I guess it was my own fault. When I was serving on the Mother's Group board, I tried to lay low by serving as the secretary—the number four mom in charge. But our president was too shy to speak in front of groups, so I often made announcements at our monthly meetings. And, well, I was the emcee of the annual Mother's Group egg hunt, because, after all, they gave me a bullhorn, which I used at home to announce dinner for a few days before the event. And who wouldn't say yes to that? So, it's no wonder people thought I was running the show.

At the same time, I also served on the community's recreation department committee. I tried to take on low-profile jobs like making trips to Staples to buy copy paper, but I soon found myself helping to stage a fundraising fashion show. No bullhorn there, but I did win the fifty-fifty raffle, which, of course, didn't look good, considering my name was on the "Thanks to . . ." page in the show's program. As the committee chairperson's right-hand woman, I guess that I was in charge there, too.

So I can't blame anyone but myself that an angry mob of mothers picked me to lodge their complaint about Movie Night—or the lack thereof. I'd run enough things in this town that people just assumed I'd be responsible for that, too. Even my eight-year-old neighbor once remarked, "Mrs. Singer, you're in charge of everything!"

I had to wean the community off me, one unanswered phone call at a time.

The Usual Suspects

Why is it that the volunteers in town are often the same few people over and over? One fall, I coached not one, but two boys' soccer teams in the town's recreation department leagues. By November, I figured I'd done my share of coaching for the school year, but no. My soccer cleats hadn't even dried out from the season when I got a phone call from a frantic dad: "Wanna coach basketball?"

Uh, no. I'm happy to explain offsides to a bunch of kids (and parents) who don't know a goal kick from a sidekick, but I'm not going to coach a sport I played for just three years back in junior high school, not when I've got thirty years of soccer under my belt (or rather, in my cleats). Besides, if there were ten kids on each second-grade basketball team, and six teams altogether, where were the fifty-nine other parents?

Eventually, he found a coach for my son's team—his baseball coach.

No wonder it's always the usual suspects as the coaches, class parents, club presidents, fundraising chairs, and volunteers. We answer our phones. And we don't know how to just say "no." But as important as it might make us feel, it's really not fair. And it's not always fun.

Last soccer season, the referee didn't show up for our big semifinal playoff game. The other team's coach shrugged, looked at me, and said, "You know more about the rules than I do." And that's how I wound up reffing my team's playoff game in the mud with no cleats or sports bra. Luckily, my assistant coach took over coaching the team, because I couldn't very well shout, "Jake! Pass it to Andy!" while making calls. As it turns out, some of my calls were unpopular.

A few minutes into the game, a kid on the other team had a hand ball inside the penalty box. It wasn't an accidental hand ball, like when the ball sorta swipes your hand, or I'd have let it go. This was two hands over his head smacking at the ball, as though a volleyball game had suddenly broken out in the middle of the soccer playoffs. So I blew my whistle and called a penalty kick, which, according to FIFA, soccer's governing body, is the correct call. As a result, a player from my team went up against their goalie one-on-one and scored.

Apparently, this didn't sit well with the parents on the other side of the field, because five minutes later, when I called a free kick for the other team because one of my own players spiked the ball outside the penalty box with his hands, a father of the opposing team shouted to their coach, "Hey Mike! Is that a penalty kick, too?"

Oh how I wanted to yell, "No it's not a penalty kick because it's not in the penalty box, Mr. Smarty Pants. Go home and look it up. Oh, and the sideline is not a sound-proof force field. I CAN HEAR YOU!" But I was too busy trying to ref the game and not fall flat on my butt in the mud. Note to self: Keep soccer cleats in the car.

A few minutes later, after I called a dangerous play on the other team's right fullback, who was sitting on the ground and kicking at the ball as though he were an extra on *Romper Room*, another father shouted, "OH, COME ON!"

Here's the whistle, pal. It's all yours. I came here to coach, but if I hadn't reffed the game, there'd be no game, and you and the other fifty people on the sideline could take your kids and go home until the snow covers the field for the winter.

Perhaps the usual suspects always volunteer because then we don't have anything to complain about.

Shine That Spotlight Over Here, Please

When I was the secretary of the Mother's Group, I had a small but loyal following who loved my ramblings in the community newsletter. Some of them were even mothers. One of my neighbors, a grandmother who presumably had no interest in the goings-on of the Mother's Group, which caters to moms of kids under age six, told me she found my announcements about the annual Red, White, and Blue bike parade "entertaining" and my recounting of the Fall Festival "well written." To me, her comments were as exciting as a favorable *New York Times* book review.

Even the head of the community's maintenance department—the guys who clear snow from the roads in winter and set up the swim lanes at the lake in May—was a fan of my Mother's Group column. And that sure came in handy when we needed a new set of equipment installed at the playground.

At the time, the Mother's Group's section of the newsletter was the only regular outlet for my writing. I'd published a few magazine articles, but mostly I spent my days trying to keep objects out of my boys' noses and rescuing the cat from four grubby, tail-pulling hands. As a result, the newsletter was my spotlight, albeit a brief, biweekly one.

For many moms, volunteering is the only way to get this kind of much-needed recognition. Nobody's going to ask you to stand for a round of applause at dinner because you managed to save your baby's Binkie from falling down the drain in the supermarket parking lot. But they'll publicly thank you for wrapping 157 gift baskets for the school fundraiser. Finally, a pat on the back. And it's worth it, even if you had to pull two all-nighters to get the job done.

So we volunteer even when we don't really have the time, if for nothing else but to hear the words "Thank you," more often than just when we pass the ketchup. I know, I know. We're not mothers for the recognition. But after all those sleepless nights, blow-out diapers, and the sacrifices we make for our kids, I know I've started to wonder if I'm doing a good job. Most of the time, nobody tells me so.

What's more, motherhood exhausted me while volunteering rejuvenated me. I once calculated the number of nights of interrupted sleep I'd endured when my kids were very little. By the time my younger son slept through the night—at sixteen months old—I figure I'd had about 850 consecutive nights of someone waking me up for something or another. And boy was I tired.

So tired, in fact, that when some friends and my husband started bragging about their work achievements, I got a little punchy. One announced he'd gotten a promotion. One said she was given an award. My husband mentioned his raise. I blurted, "I'm really good at sleep deprivation!" and collapsed onto the couch in giggles while they ignored me and compared plaques or bonuses or whatever corporate people do. Oh, how I needed a pat on the back.

No wonder I put so much into volunteering. It was the only place where I was sure I was succeeding. I knew this because other people told me so. In fact, they still call me about it today. But now, I don't answer the phone.

10 Signs You Over-Volunteer Just a Tad

1. There's no room in the trunk of your car for groceries because it's filled with four hundred plastic Easter eggs for next weekend's community egg hunt.
2. You have time to fold, label, and stuff into bags enough T-ball jerseys and hats for the entire league, but your dirty laundry is spilling out of all the hampers in the house.
3. Nineteen of the last twenty "Recent Calls" listed on your cell phone were from your co-chair for the fall festival.
4. The other call was from the petting zoo folks who need to know if you really want goats after last year's "That thing is eating my daughter's skirt!" debacle.
5. You own a generator, and you know how to hook it up to a microphone, an Italian ice machine, and a bouncy castle without blowing a fuse.
6. You keep a loaded glue gun in your glove compartment.
7. People in town just automatically assume they should send sign-up sheets and checks to you, even if your name isn't on the flyer.
8. You have enough cupcake tins to supply dessert for a party in the U.S. Senate.

9. You were in school so much this year, most kindergarteners thought you were a teacher. And so did the janitors. And the music teacher.

10. You don't need make-up because you've got glitter glue all over your hands and face much of the time anyhow.

Swimming with the Sharks

In some communities, the top volunteer jobs are cluttered with über moms who are in it for the status. To these mothers, serving as the head class mom is much like running a department at Microsoft's headquarters and reporting to Bill Gates himself. Running the spring Tricky Tray fundraiser is akin to organizing a new administration's inaugural ball, and the PTA presidency is akin to being governor of the state. The only thing that's missing is the limo waiting outside school.

These moms don't just volunteer to help the teacher for an hour. They spend fifteen minutes of that hour trying to sell the teacher on a new math system they read about in *Education Week*. They don't stop in simply to laminate "What I'm Thankful For" placemats for the class, they also sign up to aide (aka spy on) lunchtime, help the art teacher paint props for the class play, and drop by the principal's office to discuss proper playground etiquette and how Dylan Macaluso isn't following it when it comes to their daughters.

In short, they want to rule the school, if not the whole town and perhaps a small serfdom.

While all volunteers want to help better the school or the community, the über-volunteers want to better it *for themselves and their children,* and screw everybody else. If Amelia can get a better shot of winning a prize at the preschool Halloween costume parade because Mommy's in charge, well, Mommy'd better sign up. And if Tyler can get more playing time if Mom coaches kiddie soccer, Mom had better volunteer to coach even if all she knows about soccer is that David Beckham plays it, and boy, is he cute!

Besides, that's why she spent all that money on a private goalie coach for her six-year-old in the first place.

Jen's Tips for Volunteering Without Losing Your Mind
Volunteer to See Your Kids

Pick volunteer jobs that bring you closer to your kids, rather than closer to some committee that meets during your kid's football games.

I confess: I am a serial class mom. I have served as a class mom for at least one of my boy's classes for the past four years, and I just signed up again for next year. But as volunteer jobs go, this one lets me spend more time with my sons while allowing me to see how they act at school (it's often much more polite than the way they act at home).

Plus, I get to see which kid is trouble (i.e., the child who's stuffing little pieces of paper into a hole in his teacher's desk while she isn't looking) and which to block from our phone when my sons start dating (i.e., the girl in the leopard print miniskirt and belly shirt who keeps finding excuses to tackle the boys on the playground).

My kids like it because it makes them feel important when the teacher says, "Everybody say thank you to Mrs. Singer for helping us make picture frames today." Plus, they know I'll make sure to bring their favorite juice to the Valentine's Day party.

I like it because I like kids, especially mine. And there's just something about taking an hour out of your day to eat cupcakes (or health-conscious oatmeal raisin cookies, as far as the principal knows), read books, and play games. You just don't get much of that when you're a grown-up (although I did come close to it when I worked in advertising).

Sticking to volunteer jobs like class mom, soccer coach, and timing the swim lanes at races works for me—because I get to help out without leaving my kids. I try to avoid volunteering for anything that takes time away from my family, such as fundraiser chair, school board representative, recreation department head, home and school association president, and anything that requires me to spend more than fifteen minutes a week at Staples.

Just Say No

If you don't want to organize the Cub Scouts popcorn sale, simply say, "No thanks." You don't need to provide a reason why you don't want 213 giant tins of popcorn in your garage. Why do you think the person who's asking you to do it isn't clearing out her garage in the first place?

If you say no enough times, you'll drop from the top of the Sucker List—the list of tried-and-true volunteers who can't say no. Don't worry. Someone else *will* take your place. That might make you feel unneeded, but as soon as you realize you won't be the one catching grief because someone bought acrylic (aka "Damn, this stuff doesn't come out of my good shirt!") paints for the spin art sets, you'll get over it.

Just say no to volunteer jobs that take you away from your kids too much, annoy your spouse ("Honey, when are these 139 boxes of Thin Mints getting out of our living room?"), or overwhelm you. If you hate math, just say no to "Would you serve as treasurer this year?" If you despise writing, just say no to "Will you keep the minutes at the meeting?"

The same goes for the smaller, temporary jobs. If you're going on a business trip this week, don't sign up to bring the snacks to Friday night's football game. No one thinks you're a Super Mom for buying up all the Cinnamon Chip Scones and lemonades at the airport Starbucks because that's all you had time for. At $2.25 a muffin and three bucks for each lemonade, you're not a Super Mom, you're an idiot.

Be the Boss

Why would you want to be the head class mom rather than an assistant? Isn't that more work? Not if you do it right. I mentioned earlier that you can assign a Super Mom to take on volunteer duties you hate to do. Even better, when you're the boss you can schedule class parties around your calendar and choose the responsibilities you prefer. You don't see Donald Trump checking up on the tasks at Burger King on *The Apprentice.* He's got his peeps for that, and if you're in charge, you do, too.

Yet when you're the top volunteer, it's very important that you don't take on the role of garbage collector. You know the drill: If no one else will bake 325 cupcakes/ask the local chiropractor for a donation/pick out and pick up one thousand temporary tattoos/print out the snack sign-up sheet/buy the teacher's gift/schedule every swim meet for the next three months, you will. And everyone knows it. So your committee, your neighbors, and the moms at school pickup stay mum when you look for volunteers, expecting you to pick up the slack.

Instead, you have to show up for the first meeting looking super busy and acting like a bit of a hard-ass. Bring a clipboard or one of those jumbo file folders with a Velcro close, a cup of coffee (grande, of course), and a PDA, which you keep frantically checking even though all you're really getting is some spam and a couple of lame jokes about al-Qaeda forwarded by your brother.

When no one takes up the job of, say, stapling five hundred programs for the annual Summer Fun Festival, ask, "Who'd like to oversee the porta-potty delivery?" Suddenly, you'll have three volunteers for the program-stapling, which will take hours, leaving you to spend just seven minutes before the big event pointing at a clearing near the woods and shouting, "Put it there!"

It's good to be the boss.

Want to Be Class Mom?

NAME: _____ ADDRESS: _____

HOME PHONE: _____(so we can call you at an ungodly hour to tell you that school is canceled due to snow that hasn't even started falling yet)

WORK PHONE: _____(so we can call you in the middle of your performance review)

CELL PHONE: _____ (so we can call you for your opinion on Halloween crafts while you're trapped in the bank drive-through lane with a howling baby)

Have you ever applied for and/or served as class mom before?
    YES   NO

If yes, choose all that apply:

_____ I served as Head Class Mom, in charge of the other mothers and their questionable crafting skills.

_____ I attended the class trip, even though I had the flu, my minivan had a flat tire and I'm allergic to petting zoos.

_____ I now know better than to wear cashmere while helping the class make menorahs with finger paint.

_____ I promise to read the directions on the laminating machine this time.

_____ I did not lose the class pet hamster over the holiday break, no matter what the other moms say.

Do you have any special training, skills or expertise? (Check all that apply):

____ I'm the fastest glue gunner this side of the Mississippi.

____ I know the words to "The Wheels on the Bus"—all twelve verses.

____ I used to work in crowd control for the police department.

____ I have an in at Prada, and I'd like to be in charge of the teacher's gift.

What do you hope to get out of the class mom position?

____ I hope to beat the school's current record for most cookies baked in one semester.

____ I hope to get to talk to grown-ups.

____ I hope to find out what my twins do when they're not at home ganging up on the cat.

____ I hope to discover where my son puts the carrot sticks I pack as his snack, because he's too hungry after school to have eaten them.

How did you hear about the class mom position? (Check all that apply):

____ I've been waiting for this opportunity ever since my baby was born.

____ While eavesdropping in line at the supermarket.

____ In the thirteen fliers sent home since the first day of school.

____ Oh, I thought this was the form for the fifty-fifty raffle.

____ The other moms put me up to it, because they don't want to make gingerbread houses out of milk cartons.

Originally appeared in *Parenting* magazine.

SECRET FOUR

You Didn't Invent Motherhood

She was trying hard to humor me, pretending I was telling her vital information, such as how to jump-start her car in a bad neighborhood at 4 a.m., rather than giving her instructions on how to feed a baby. My mother-in-law was about to take care of my firstborn, Nicholas, then eight months old, for an entire weekend—the first time my husband and I were to take a much-needed vacation from parenting a sleepless baby.

I gave her detailed instructions on feeding, changing, sleeping, and entertaining her grandson, speaking as though she were a new hire unaccustomed to the way my office worked. I stopped short of pointing out where my baby's mouth was, but my Nervous New Mother Orientation Session probably sounded that ridiculous to her, a thirty-four-year veteran mom.

After I left, I sobbed the whole way home. I would miss him terribly, of course, but I also feared something bad might happen while under my in-laws' care. You'd think I'd just left him with a bunch of tweens trying on low-riders at Abercrombie & Fitch instead of with two people who had raised three children—and in the sixties and seventies, no less, when they didn't even have baby monitors or wipe warmers.

Two years later, when I dropped off my younger son for his first overnight visit, I handed my mother-in-law the diaper bag and the baby and wished her well, as though I were leaving behind a parakeet instead of my child. This time, I didn't cry the whole way home. Rather, I sang, jamming out to any tune on the radio that had the word "party" in it, and calling friends on my cell phone to leave the message, "I'm going to get some sleep!" Party on, Mom. Party on.

What had changed? Somewhere between preparing the itemized list of my first baby's day and doing a cursory dump of my second baby's diaper bag, I realized that my mother-in-law had once managed three children under age three and—prepare yourself—with just *one* car, which my father-in-law took to work every day. She had no video baby monitor, no VCR, no DVD player, no Pack 'n' Play, no super deluxe diaper bag with the pull-out baby changing pad and personalized portable wipe holder, and no stow-and-go double stroller with cup holders.

In short, my mother-in-law was a parenting superstar. She knew what she was doing, and, outside of some instructions on medication and food preferences, she really didn't need me, a new mother, to tell her how to take care of a baby for forty-eight hours.

But like many mothers of this generation, I assumed I knew more about motherhood, because, darn it, I had read *What to Expect the First Year*, I had passed a baby CPR class, and I had watched plenty of *Oprah*, who assured me that "parenting is the toughest job on earth."

Once I got over myself, though, I trusted my mother-in-law and other people to take care of my children. And that brought with it great freedom. Also, sleep. It just took a while to get there.

Invention One: I'm the Only One Who Can Care for My Children

I was in a Bed, Bath, and Beyond store with my mother and my kids when another mother shouted at her son, "Stay where I can see you!" My mom pointed out that things were different when I was little. Back then, she never feared someone would snatch me from the fingertip towel aisle.

Certainly, our generation of mothers is more safety-conscious than our moms were, and with good reason. But somehow we extrapolated the need to watch our children more closely into the idea that only we are capable of caring for our kids, and that's simply not true.

When I was a full-time stay-at-home mom, I treated my 24/7 role as a job I took very seriously. So seriously, in fact, that I felt that any time I wasn't fully engaging my children in brain-building activities, I wasn't doing my job well. I rushed back from haircuts and doctor's appointments as though any extra time spent, say, stopping to buy myself a banana and strawberry smoothie was wasting away my kids' childhood. After all, I wasn't with them, and, apparently, spending any less than the one hundred hours a week I typically cared for them was a waste. Or so I thought. It was *my* job, after all, not someone else's.

I had fooled myself into believing I was more needed than I was, and, naturally, that made me feel important. I remember stepping into the garage to put something in the recycling bin while my two toddlers banged on the door, crying. I was gone, what, maybe thirty seconds tops? But my babies needed me! Me, and only me! I am mother, hear me roar!

Yet what they really needed was to see that other people besides Mommy could take care of them, and that Mommy sometimes goes away, but she always comes back. Sometimes it's even longer than thirty seconds, and everybody survives. How about that?

After I realized that my mother-in-law was capable of caring for my kids, I started to trust other people, including my husband, friends, babysitters, and my own mother. While letting other people watch my kids allowed me to enjoy such freedoms as trying on pants without a pint-sized audience climbing under the dressing room stalls, it was also good for my children. They had fun playing with (aka getting spoiled by) their grandparents. Plus, our teenage babysitter had way more patience for making Play-Doh balls of poop than I did.

Invention Two: My Husband Is a Clueless Man Who Can't Even Pack a Diaper Bag Without Supervision

My father changed one diaper during his entire life, and somehow lived to tell about it. He can recall some forty years later just how horrific that experience was for him, the poor man. But to his generation, I'm sure he was considered a hero. He changed a diaper! And it was poopy! Congratulations, Dad.

We expect more of today's fathers, who usually change way more than just one of the average 2,500 diapers a baby goes through in a year. And yet, when they fall short of our (often ridiculously high) expectations, we assume they're the useless clods we've seen fathers portrayed as on TV (i.e., *The King of Queens, Everybody Loves Raymond*) and in the movies (i.e., *Daddy Day Care* and the classic Dad-is-clueless film, *Mr. Mom*).

I often grew impatient when my husband didn't whip up a bottle of formula or calm a crying kid down as fast or as well as I could. And by "grow impatient," I mean, of course, that I'd roll my eyes and emit a pained sigh like a thirteen-year-old who has to show Mom yet again how to log onto the Internet.

Never mind that I had done these things numerous times a day while he was at work, to the point where I could diaper two kids faster than a Macy's gift-wrapper can bedeck your presents in red and green ribbons on December 24.

Yet if I had tried to do something in his office for the first time, I'd be slow at it, too. When you are the primary caregiver, expecting your husband to be as proficient at parenting as you are is like putting your grandmother up against Jeff Gordon in the Daytona 500 and shouting, "C'mon, Grandma! Put the pedal to the metal!" You can swaddle a baby and administer bubble gum-flavored Motrin in your sleep because you've done it over and over again. He, however, needs to take that learning curve you sped around (while opening the stroller with one hand and holding a squirming baby with the other) a little more carefully. So why not let him?

Why not? Because it makes you feel indispensable when your husband can't keep up with your obviously superior parenting skills, that's why. You're like Matt Damon in *The Bourne Supremacy*, when he kills two CIA agents and downloads their cell phone data in less than a minute without even breaking a sweat before driving off with one agent's car. You're efficient. You're quick. And there's no one quite like you.

But your husband really doesn't have to be just like you to do a decent job of caring for your kids. Perfectly good is good enough. Let him spend a few hours changing poopy diapers while you go out and buy some cute shoes, maybe even for yourself. Then you won't have to hear about his diaper-of-a-lifetime forty years from now.

10 Reasons Your Mother Is More Than Qualified to Watch Your Kids

1. She used cloth diapers—fastening safety pins with one hand—back before it was an eco-chic choice. (In other words, she had no choice.)

2. She managed to keep your grubby little hands out of her hairspray-shellacked hairdo that was freshly coiffed every week.

3. She had two kids before the double baby jogger was invented. (But, how did she work out?)

4. She survived the Great Temper Tantrum of 1972, involving you and a box of Captain Crunch she didn't have a coupon for.

5. She knows where the hospital is located and she can drive.

6. She has a few dozen years more experience at parenting than you do.

7. The poor woman had to wear maternity clothes with big pink bows on them, and yet still she went out in public.

8. She was able to move about the house during your naptime, even though she didn't have video baby monitors set up in each room, like you do.

9. She's been shopping at Baby Gap again. It doesn't qualify her to watch the kids, but it does save you lots of money.

10. She's still faster than a speeding toddler.

Google "Parenting" and You Could Spend Hours Sifting Through Overwhelming and Terrifying Information

When I was pregnant with my second son, I Googled "pre-term labor" and "high risk" and found a wonderful listserv for expecting mothers like me who had experienced pre-term labor with previous pregnancies and were, therefore, considered high-risk for giving birth to another pre-term baby. I wanted to find out all that I could about pre-term labor, because I had spent the end of July managing to thwart the birth of this baby, who was due November 1.

But I also found websites that scared the bejesus out of me, citing statistics that warned I was even more likely to give birth to a preemie the second time around, leaving me panicked, wondering who would take care of my toddler while I commuted to the hospital to visit my baby in the NICU. Every ache or odd feeling sent me reeling, frantically Googling words like "birth at twenty-eight weeks" and "birth at twenty-eight-and-a-half weeks" and "birth at twenty-nine weeks."

In the end, my second baby was born full-term eleven weeks after he'd first tried to show up. And here I'd gone and put family and friends on alert (and on an elaborate caregiving schedule "just in case") for nothing.

One of the greatest advantages of modern mothering is our access to a seemingly unlimited supply of parenting information. Also, one of the biggest disadvantages of modern mothering is our access to a seemingly unlimited supply of parenting information. As I turned to the parenting experts and the surplus of "It happened to me" stories on the Internet more and more, I relied on my own gut less and less.

If only I'd just listened to Dr. Spock, who wrote in his legendary 1946 book, *Baby and Child Care*, "Trust yourself. You know more than you think you do." Our mothers did just that. Okay, so they also let us roll around seatbelt-less in the back of their station wagons as we tried to get the driver of the 80,000-pound Mac truck five feet from the car's back window to honk his horn. But they also seemed more at ease with their parenting skills than we've ever permitted ourselves to be. Perhaps that's because they trusted themselves.

I'm not saying information is necessarily a bad thing. When my son was diagnosed with reflux as a baby, I read up on it, so I would understand our pediatrician's treatment plan. But when my Internet search dug up scary stories about babies with the same digestive disorder who couldn't hold down enough food to keep them from losing weight, I turned off my computer. My son was gaining weight rather nicely, thank you. (Twenty-five pounds by a year old. "Please learn to walk.") There was no reason to get myself all worked up about what could happen, tearfully reading sad stories from frustrated mothers with sicker kids and alarming medical abstracts about worst-case scenarios.

What twenty-first-century mom-to-be didn't start out reading about fetal distress and vanishing twin syndrome (Oh. My. God. What is *that?*) in that unnerving section on what could go wrong in *What to Expect When You're Expecting?* I know I did, which is why I know way too much about uterine rupture, which occurs in fewer than five in one thousand pregnancies and in neither of mine.

It took me until I finished *What to Expect: The Toddler Years* to learn to use such books as a reference guide for various issues, rather than as a study guide for potential mothering pop quizzes. By then, I'd done a fine job of driving myself a bit insane.

Jen's Tips for Letting Go So You Can Shop Without Your Restless Entourage in Bob the Builder Sneakers
Demote Yourself from The Great Nurturer to The Perfectly Fine Mom

Becoming a mother is a little like suddenly stepping into Oprah's shoes: You're powerful, you're needed, and you're one-of-a-kind. It's a heady time when you can easily become drunk with the power of being the household's It Girl, the end-of-the-line authority on the children, the house, and all that's in it. Your decisions outweigh everyone else's simply because you're the mother. You are the top dog, and everyone knows it, especially you.

My husband must think so, too, as he defers many major parenting decisions to me because I'm the mom. Also, because I'm the one who has read all the parenting books, researched everything from instilling good study skills to children's baseball mitts, and interviewed other mothers about the pros and cons of such issues as whether to sign the kids up for the local swim team and which third-grade teachers are the best.

It doesn't matter whether you're home with the kids all day or at a job elsewhere, Mom is usually the planner, the scheduler, the organizer, and the person who wonders if there are any more Pokémon lunch boxes still left at Target. If you ask my husband which days the kids have library at school, he'd have no idea. I, on the other hand, will have not only memorized their school schedules, but likely also will have been searching since Tuesday for the soon-to-be overdue book, *Time Warp Trio: Viking It and Liking It.*

Yet, here's the dirty little secret about being the person in charge: The more you take on, the more your family relies on you for everything from keeping track of where their extra shoelaces are to making sure they have enough of those pretzels they like to snack on while playing Monopoly.

It takes a while to wean them off the Mom Drug, but it's oh-so-worth-it, especially on the first day you witness your children taking charge instead of standing by the door, flipping through *Ranger Rick* magazine and shouting, "Mom? Where's my backpack?"

You can start small, and you can start them young. Here's how:

1. **Don't rush to help.** Every time you drop everything to help your baby find the toy she wants to shove in her mouth, you teach her that you're her very own roadie. Extrapolate that out twelve years, and before you know it, you're programming her buddies' numbers into your tween's phone and driving her homework to school . . . again.

2. **Be a little more useless.** Even if you know the butter is

on the top shelf of the fridge next to the jam, don't reach in and hand it to your kids (or your husband). Just keep appearing to be engrossed in that article on campaign finance reform in the newspaper until they find the damn butter themselves. Eventually, they'll stop asking and you can save that energy for, say, buttering your toast.

3. **Be inaccessible.** Every now and then, it's good for the kids to get the proverbial busy signal when they call for Mom. Don't answer every, "Moooooom!" If they truly need you, they'll come find you.

Train a Few Second-in-Commands

Whenever the President of the United States has to undergo anesthesia, the White House holds a press conference. A spokesperson announces that while the leader of the free world is undergoing a colonoscopy, the Vice President will be in charge.

For the next few hours, everybody pretty much forgets that someone else is temporarily running the country until the same spokesperson holds another press conference to announce that the President's polyps were removed with little incident and that he is now back in the Oval Office.

I've left my children in the care of other people with more fanfare. All that was missing was the row of TV cameras and the cadre of journalists.

Maybe it was a little bit overboard to alert all the neighbors within three houses in all directions that our babysitter would be watching the children while I stepped out to cash in an expiring gift certificate for a massage. But you can't turn on your cell phone in the spa! And what if one of my children fell on the driveway and gashed his head on the rocks, and then the babysitter twisted her ankle trying to get to him, and then it started raining so hard that passers-by couldn't see what was going on and call 911?

Frankly, it doesn't matter how neurotic you seem when you prepare to turn over caring for your kids to someone else, as long as it makes you feel comfortable enough to emit that long, relieving sigh when you shut the door and leave. You are simply training someone else to fill in for you in a way that makes it possible for you to give up your reign, if only for a short while.

The more trained second-in-commands you have on call, the more opportunities you have to leave your house without packing up your brood and dragging them to your OB/GYN appointment. (If you haven't tried to keep an inquisitive three-year-old "over here by Mommy's head," you may not yet understand how useful a good fill-in is when it's time for your annual pap smear.)

Give your temporary replacement more information than they'll probably ever need. Leave an emergency contact number for everyone, not just for your cell phone, but also for the paramedic who lives down the street. Give them their own Vanna White demonstration of baby monitors, swings, food preparation, home-work supervision, Nintendo—whatever makes *you* happy. Then close the door and let out that sigh. You are no longer in charge. For now.

Shorten Your Back Fence: Create an Adjustable Board of Advisors That Provides Most of Your Parenting Information

All I wanted was to find out how to treat my son's eczema. I had set up an appointment with his pediatrician, but I wanted to go into the office with as much information as possible so that my child would get the best care possible. At least, that's what I told myself when I found myself skimming through medical abstracts with seven-syllable words and a dozen lines of references in four-point type on obscure research websites at 2 a.m.

Soon enough, I started to both understand and worry about this sort of thing: "A variety of hypotheses may help to explain the participation of IgE antibodies in the induction of eczema: vaso-active media." Considering that my college degree had little to do with medicine save the five days I spent in the infirmary with strep throat and the self-treatment of a few killer hangovers, that's pretty impressive.

Though I didn't learn much that would help my son that night, I did diagnose my own problem: a raging case of TMI—Too Much Information. Also, NES—Not Enough Sleep. And when you're a mom, the combination of the two can be dangerous.

While our mothers relied on pediatricians, Dr. Spock, Grandma, and the other carpool moms for their parenting information, we twenty-first-century moms have a virtual ocean of information available to us. And it's easy to get pulled into the riptide. But if you learn to do a little information triage, you can find what you need quickly and easily without getting sucked into the wrong end of the back fence.

I've narrowed my pool of parenting information into three main areas, so that I don't wind up combing the four-point type after midnight ever again. They include the following:

1. **Parents who've done the research already.** You can cut down on your research time considerably by finding parents who have already been there, done that. Whether they're in your neighborhood or on an Internet message board, seek out parents who have already tamed the Terrible Two's, picked a soccer camp for aspiring goalies, treated ADHD, or staged a MySpace intervention. It'll save you loads of time sifting out the unnecessary information among the gems.

2. **Published information with credibility and good editing.** Bookmark a few well-known medical and parenting information sites you can rely on for background information.

Chances are, these sites won't be riddled with typos, links to naked Britney Spears photos, or pop-up ads with dancing silhouettes touting low mortgage rates. Most quality books will be printed by established publishers, or its author will have a good reputation in his or her industry.

3. **Mom and other confidants who will help you get a reality check.** Whether it's a cousin, the doctor, or your mom who raised four kids, make sure there's someone you can call when you're not sure if you should phone the pediatrician or if you need to schedule a meeting with your child's math teacher.

While You Were Out, Mom

- Your toddler stood at the back door sobbing for about forty-five seconds and then went back to stuffing tissues between the couch cushions.
- Grandma sugared up the kids again. They'll peak just when *Desperate Housewives* comes on tonight.
- Nobody let the cat in.
- Daddy helped himself to the banana bread. You know, the one you made for tomorrow's bake sale?
- Nobody noticed the juice box straw on the floor. They just stepped over it again and again and again.
- The baby ate all her strained peas and took a two-and-a-half-hour nap. But face it: She'll never do that for you.
- Somebody called. Uh, Janet? Jane? Or was it Jean? I know! Jan! It was Jan! I think. . . . Do you know a Jan?
- The cat started picking at the sliding screen door with her claws, and yet no one let her in.

- The vacuum continued its peaceful nap in the closet next to the mop.
- Somebody broke your favorite aromatherapy candle and tried to glue it back together with chewed gum.
- The cat made a hole in the screen door big enough to get her front paw and her head through, and still no one let her in.
- The sitter talked on her cell phone the whole time. By the way, what's a "thong"?
- Your mother called and wanted to know what that noise was in the background. She said it sounded like someone was banging toy trucks on the kitchen table. How did she know that?
- We watched *Chitty Chitty Bang Bang*—all two hours and twenty minutes of it—and now that you're home, we need to burn off some nervous energy.
- Hey! How did the cat get in?
- We sure missed you!

Originally appeared in *Parenting* magazine.

Your Kid's Birthday Party Isn't Your Coming-Out Celebration

We heard the music as soon as we turned the corner. A big party was happening that gorgeous summer day, so my husband and I pushed our sons down the street in our double stroller to see who was having the bash. As we got closer, we saw two large white tents—one for the band and dance floor and one for the elaborate barbecue set-up. We could hear kids shouting with joy as they jumped into the pool. Someone announced over the microphone that the ribs were ready.

Maybe it's a big engagement party or a fiftieth birthday bash, I thought. But children's "Happy Birthday" balloons had been tied to the mailbox. Next to the pool sat one rather large bouncy castle—the kind of bouncy castle you might get to see once a year at a traveling carnival or at a charity event for a children's hospital. And that's when it hit me: This was a birthday party for a *child*.

Dumbstruck, I stopped the stroller and stared. The band—yes, a live band—started playing *Glory Days*. My husband turned to me and said, "Look, honey! They've even got Springsteen!"

Glory days indeed. How did they think they'd top that birthday party the next year? Lollapalooza? Live Aid? Woodstock?

It's no secret that children's birthday parties have gotten out of hand, what with the backyards full of pony rides, rock climbing walls, and "naturalists" (because nowadays, every kid needs to pet a boa constrictor on his birthday).

Parents say it's for the kids, but it's also about them. It's their way of saying, "Look what great parents we are! We've got Xtreme Paintball in our yard! I bet you can't beat that."

The same goes for our kids' achievements. Surely, if Junior has been selected for the gifted program at school, it must be because of all those flashcards you taught him multiplication with back in preschool. Or if your kid's baseball team wins the championship, you get a high-five for driving him to games three times a week.

I must admit that when my son's team won the Junior Boys' Baseball League championship, I felt like blasting Queen's *We Are the Champions* and doing donuts in the parking lot with my minivan. For a moment, I even considered mounting his trophy on the hood. But I soon snapped out of it. This wasn't about me. It was about him. He won. I just watched.

That's the thing today's parents often forget: Our superior parenting skills are not what's in the spotlight. It's not about you. It's about a bunch of kids scoring more runs than the kids on the other team. It's about your child working hard in school. It's about your kid's sixth birthday. It's about your little one earning a black belt. And, no, you don't get to write the acceptance speech.

It's Not Your Trophy

No matter what the other parents say or what you might think, your kid's piano recital is not your coming-out party. It isn't your chance to show off your beautiful new dress or to showcase the fabulous job you've done raising your kids.

While it's certainly okay to feel proud of your children, it's not okay to live vicariously through their achievements, vindicating the wrongs and the near-misses of your childhood. In other words, just because you got cut from the high school basketball team, it doesn't mean that your son's MVP award belongs on your desk at work next to your "Top Salesperson, 2005" paperweight.

When my son won a trophy for Most Improved Swimmer during his first year on the swim team, I welled up with tears at the end-of-summer picnic and award ceremony. Was I proud because I'd been the one to sign him up, drive him to meets, and make sure his swim team sweatshirt made it home from practice in a sandy ball on the floor of my car?

No, I was proud because the only reason he had joined the swim team was because he didn't want to sit around waiting for his brother—who had truly wanted to join the team—to race at swim meets. At nine years old, my first-born raced against kids who had been swimming for up to three years already, some of them year-round. He barely knew how to do the breaststroke, and his racing dive was more of a modified leap, complete with nose-holding. But he swam, and he stuck with it.

So when he walked toward me that night carrying his Most Improved Swimmer trophy, I was proud that he'd truly accomplished something in an era when kids get ribbons just for showing up. I wasn't proud of me. All I'd accomplished was learning how to use the stopwatch during races and remembering to pack sunscreen for the back of my legs on sunny days, a lesson I learned when I burned them during the first race of the season. And we parents had all done just that. This trophy was all his.

You Are More Than Any One Part of You

Mr. Rogers said it and it's true: "You are more than any one part of you." While it may seem admirable to put your all into your kids, they will leave you one day, saddling you with nothing to do—unless you have other hobbies and interests, not to mention friends. Also, self-esteem.

Soon after the first "Baby on Board" sign was affixed to a window of, most likely, a 1985 Volvo, parenting made a shift that could have scored a 7.5 on the Richter scale. Motherhood went from "Just wait until your father gets home" to "Now, Giana. You shouldn't pull the cat's tail. That's not nice. How about we redirect your energy by making pretty wall stickers out of contact paper and rainbow-colored paints?"

We switched from authoritarian to democratic parenting, from in charge to on the verge of out of control. And we did it because we thought it was best for our kids. Because they're *special*. The teachers said so at preschool. And kindergarten. And Little League. And the summer reading program in the park. And at the bank drive-through window. And even at "Kids eat free on Tuesdays!" Hooters.

We have a very special job raising these very special children, so we'd darn well better take it seriously. And we'd better make it our number one priority, even over our personal hygiene and lunch. But all that focus on our kids isn't just bad for them, it's bad for Mom, too.

In the middle of all that floor time and all those Mommy and Me classes, I lost myself. Which is why when I heard Mr. Rogers sing on TV, "You are more than any one part of you," I burst into tears. I wasn't more than any one part of me. I was Mommy, and I had the Play-Doh birthday cakes and cardboard box castles, complete with functioning drawbridge, to prove it. I had sippy cups rolling under my feet while I drove my car, and new clothes for both boys while I wore the same khaki pants with holes in the knees from dropping to the ground to play Vroom! Vroom! trucks over and over again.

I knew an excavator from a backhoe, but I couldn't identify any of the non-animated films listed on the marquee outside the movie theater in my town. I could rattle off the price of a jumbo box of diapers, but I had no idea how much lipstick cost. I could tell you what time *Blues Clues* came on TV, but not who was sitting in the anchor chair on the evening news. (Where *did* Tom Brokaw go?)

So I sat on the couch with my two toddlers on my lap, quietly sobbing while Mr. Rogers sang about the many parts of me that I had completely forgotten about. Like the part that used to play tennis and the part that used to go out to dinner with grown-ups. Oh, and the part that used to shave my legs on a regular basis. Though it took years to snap out of it, I started to be more than just a mom, little by little. Turns out, it was better not just for me, but for my kids, too.

As my children got older, they learned that the world didn't revolve around them like two pint-sized suns radiating energy and providing life and purpose for everyone around them. I didn't stop putting them first altogether, but they became more of a headline band to other worthy warm-up bands of mine, like a hot shower, breakfast, the *New York Times*, and grown-up clothes.

Finally, I became more than any one part of me—especially the part that parents.

Nobody Likes a Stage Mother

You don't have to dress your child up in frills and makeup and teach her how to tap dance to be a stage mother. You can do it alongside baseball diamonds, at weekend-long swim meets (bring your Sudoku), at cheerleading competitions a thousand miles from home (Yaaaaay team! Go frequent flyer miles!), and at spelling bees nationwide. (Plethoric. Excessively abundant. P-L-E-T-H-O-R-I-C. Plethoric.)

Never before have there been so many opportunities to immerse yourself in the world of Competitive Child-Rearing, what with travel soccer starting at age six and Piano for Peanuts aimed at kids

Mommy Was a Good Girl Today. She Deserves a Sticker.

1. I managed to find a G-rated word to shout after dropping a bottle of apple juice on my bare foot.

2. I extracted my toddler from the mall carousel without bribery, muscle power, or the kind of negotiation skills you might see on *Deal or No Deal.*

3. I saved my son's beloved blankie from falling into the large, murky puddle in the Wal-Mart parking lot.

4. I used the stop-and-go traffic I was stuck in as an opportunity to retrieve various toys, pacifiers, balled-up socks, and bottles as they rolled under my feet.

5. I didn't eat the Girl Scout cookies. Well, not all of them. Just the Thin Mints.

6. I resisted the urge to wet my thumb and wipe the mustard off my boss's otherwise white beard at lunch today.

7. I forced a smile when my mother-in-law let the baby fall asleep in her arms, effectively undermining the three weeks of sleep training I'd just endured.

8. I plucked both of my eyebrows . . . on the same day, no less.

9. I praised my husband for making the bed. (The very same bed I've made every single day with no audible acknowledgment or even a thumbs-up for seven years.)

10. I transferred a sleeping child from the car to the crib without stepping on any squeaky toys, banging my knee on the car seat, or startling the dog (thus obliterating naptime).

11. I snagged front-row seats for the hottest show in town . . . the *sold out* Wiggles concert!

12. In my car I found a safety pin, a pair of Superman underpants, three Band-Aids, Barbie's shoes, a bag of Cheerios, a Starbucks

napkin that had doubled as a tissue, change for the kiddie rides, and the school nurse's phone number. (The playgroup now calls me "MacGyver.")

13. I got the "choo-choo" to ride into the "station" over and over again, until all the broccoli was gone.

14. I found mittens at the store even though the spring fashions are already out.

15. I got a hero's welcome today, and all I'd done was step outside to get the mail.

who can't even read their own names, let alone a musical note. And guess what! *You* can be the mom behind the wunderkind! You just have to think like a spin doctor and act like a bodyguard.

When one mother from a nearby town found out that her daughter would have to repeat first grade, what did she do? She evened the playing field for her seven-year-old *by moving*. Rather than perform what she must have perceived as damage control to her child's academic reputation, she put her house up for sale and moved her family to another school district across town so her child could start fresh (and save face) in the fall. Rather than teaching her daughter to deal with life's setbacks, she reinvented her, like the Bionic Woman of elementary school: Better. Stronger. Faster. Hollywood couldn't have done it better.

Today's stage mother stands in the wings of every aspect of her children's lives, ready to do whatever it takes to build a better kid. She has sacrificed her weekends and most of her weeknights, her car (which smells like a combination of sporting event, sweat, and Doritos), and her own aspirations to read something other than a swim meet competition list that says Mom's got twenty-nine races to go until Junior's up for the Boys Eight and Under Freestyle Relay.

Maybe these moms love carting their kids from lacrosse to baseball to soccer in one day. Maybe they think they're helping create the next Michael Jordan or Mia Hamm. Or maybe they just like living out of their SUVs festooned with football helmet stickers. But when they cross the line from carpooling mom to stage mom, they're living vicariously through their kids' activities.

The stage mom, once as rare as a wild horse, is thriving among twenty-first-century parents. There are just too many opportunities to be a helicopter parent these days, hovering over your kids' every move. And it's not just parents of small children doing all that hovering. Today's stage mothers (and fathers) call their college kids every day to micromanage everything from their economics exam to what's for dinner. And it doesn't end there. Helicopter parents have even been seen at their grown children's job interviews. What's next? Overseeing their daughters' twenty-week sonograms when they're pregnant? Probably.

Jen's Tips for Not Getting Lost in Your Kid's Activities and Achievements
Think Retro

Remember your childhood birthday parties? Mine were after school, in my house, with my brother, my cousins, and a handful of friends as guests. There was no elaborately planned-out theme or goody bags worthy of the Academy Awards. Just a Carvel ice cream cake, some presents, balloons, and a piñata, and then down to the basement to listen to records and play with my brother's Rock 'Em Sock 'Em Robots. And we loved it.

I have been paring down my kids' birthday parties ever since the Great Dinosaur Party of 2003. I had rented out the local firehouse and set up crafts at several tables, where kids sat down to make soap bars with plastic dinosaurs embedded in them. (Okay, so I'm not that crafty, but it kept them sitting for at least twelve minutes.)

I was getting ready to run Duck, Duck, Goose—or rather, Raptor, Raptor, T-Rex—when one of the mothers asked, "So who's coming?" meaning, what kind of entertainment had I hired for my six-year-old's birthday party? "Um," I stammered. "That would be me."

My husband and I did our best to entertain the eighteen (aka too many) kids for the next two hours. In the end, they all wound up kicking balloons around the firehouse. "Mom!" my son shouted from amidst the balloons, "This is the funnest birthday party ever!"

And to think that after all that planning, all I really needed was a Carvel ice cream cake, some presents, a piñata, and some balloons—the same stuff I liked when I was a kid.

Don't Ignore You—or You Won't Recognize Yourself When the Kids Are Gone

There are two kinds of empty nesters: the kind who feels it's time to move on to another stage of life, and the kind who maintain their kid's room as a shrine in which they occasionally sit on the bed, clutching a stuffed animal and whimpering. If you spend eighteen years ignoring *you* so you can concentrate on your kids 100 percent, you're going to wind up the Mom who crosses off the days until Thanksgiving break at college like an inmate counting down until her parole hearing. And then you'll be sorry that you had forgotten about you.

It can be hard to concentrate on yourself when your kids are little. Their lives can consume of yours. And in these child-centric times, when you take a little time for yourself, you can feel guilty. I felt that way when my son was in junior kindergarten, and his class put on a Parent's Day show. Each kid was supposed to finish the sentence, "My mom is special because _____."

One girl said, "My mom is special because she makes me grilled cheese sandwiches." *How nice,* I thought. *They're living in an*

American cheese commercial. I can outdo that. I anxiously awaited my son's turn to praise his mother.

One boy said, "My mom is special because she hugs and kisses me." The audience said, "Awwwwwww." *Ooo, that's tough competition right there,* I thought. But surely my son would think I'm special for something similar.

Next, it was my child's turn. "My mom is special because she plays tennis." *I play tennis? I'm on the court all of an hour a week, and THAT's what he comes up with?* I forced a smile and nodded toward him. *What about MY grilled cheese sandwiches and MY hugs and kisses?* I was embarrassed.

But you know what? He was right. I *was* special, because I took time to do something that was all my own when so few mothers were doing that. And he knew it, or maybe he just thought it was cool that I could smack a tennis ball so hard. But it proved that I was more than any one part of me, because I learned not to ignore me long before my kids will leave the house for good.

Even if you have just a few hours to yourself each week, take up a hobby or an interest that's all yours. Mommy-tot yoga class is not all yours. Going out to dinner with girlfriends every third Sunday of the month, preferably at a restaurant that doesn't have a mascot, is all yours. Live your life knowing that your kids will leave you sooner than you think, and you won't lose sight of yourself again.

Keep Your Mileage Down

When my son declared himself a "cookerman," I wanted to help pave the road to his future career as a chef, so I signed him up for cooking classes—forty-five minutes from home. I'd pick him up at school and drive him to Little Chef's School, or whatever it was called, where he helped make a very tasty pumpkin bread while I endured an hour of his brother's incessant "can we go yet?"

Did I mention my little chef was in kindergarten? He could barely read, and yet, I put him in cooking classes a haul from my house.

We were stuck in traffic en route to his second class when I started to panic. *What if I don't get him to class on time?* I worried, as though I were delivering him to his final exam at the Culinary Institute of America. That's when it hit me: *Hey, I can teach him how to make pumpkin bread at home.*

Duh.

He became a cooking class dropout that day, and I became— are you ready for this?—$300 richer, thanks to the refund. I plead temporary insanity.

Keeping my mileage down by signing up for activities that are within a ten-mile/twenty-minute radius at most has helped my sanity tremendously. For example, why let the kids play travel soccer when there are numerous children who play right here in town? And why cart my kids to day camp five towns over when there's a nice science camp at the local church? Finally, why wind up in rush-hour traffic forty-five minutes from home after Little Chef class when my son could take a ($240 cheaper) cooking class in the teachers' cafeteria after school? To keep my car's mileage— and mine—down. Now you know why.

The Holiday Letter: Between the Lines

Dear friends and family,

Please pardon the form letter, but we've just been so busy *extracting my ruined Christmas cards from behind my toddler's crib* this holiday season! What with all the homemade holiday cookies *that I bought at the supermarket, but am passing off as my own,* plus the caroling we've been practicing each night

so our first-grader will stop singing "Beans, Beans" in church.
Well, the holidays are just rushing past us!
Please let it be January soon. . . . Please let it be January soon.

What a year our family had
to endure—with the four-and-a-half months of colic and
with so many exciting and unexpected events
like the cat hiding under the couch for all of September.
And the kids are getting so smart! They've figured out how to
lock the TV's remote control on The Disney Channel and
operate my digital camera to take photos of their sweet little smiles
and what appears to be the inside of the diaper pail.
We spent much of the summer at the lake, catching fireflies,
explaining why we don't keep "light-light bugs" in our sippy cups,
laughing, playing, and swimming all day long
or until we ran out of swim diapers and waterproof sunscreen.

This fall, we put Junior in school part of the day, so
I could sit down for more than three minutes at a time and
he could get some socialization in a loving environment
that hasn't caught him putting Batman stickers on the chairs yet.

I've even started a new hobby
that, so far, I've bought $400 worth of supplies for, but haven't used.
So the next time you visit, look for my new scrapbooks
collecting dust on the dining room table, along with my needlepoint.

Well, there's still so much to do to get ready for the holidays
the kids' video is over . . . and the cat's up the Christmas tree.
Happy Holidays!

If There's No White Space Left on Your Family Calendar, You've Got Too Much Going On

We were running through the parking lot with buttery bagels in our hands. My kindergartener and his best pal, Jake, were rushing to my minivan with me so we could go pick up my preschooler and then zoom over to Kiddie Soccer practice.

Stopping for bagels between kindergarten pick-up and the end of preschool after-care seemed like a great idea until we found ourselves in a long line behind very slow orderers at the bagel shop. Still, I managed to buy bagels, pick up my preschooler, race to Kiddie Soccer, help put on three pairs of shin guards and three pairs of cleats, and wipe butter off of six grubby hands.

As Jake hopped over the remains of a bagel, lying face-down on my car's floor, he said, "This car is a mess!" And then he and my boys ran onto the soccer field while I caught my breath.

He was right. My car was a mess.

And so was my calendar.

I had crammed too much into too little time and for what? My five- and six-year-old sons would have been perfectly happy spending the afternoon playing on the swings. And really, Kiddie Soccer didn't give them much of a head start on their soccer careers. (They don't play Sharks and Minnows in Major League Soccer.) And all it gave me was weekly anxiety and a big mess to clean up.

A Full Schedule Doesn't Necessarily Mean a Full Life

Sure, your kid knows how to shoot a three-pointer, do algebra (in first grade—wow!), and tie a slip knot, but when was the last time he played in his tree fort? What fort? Oh boy . . .

You don't have to be a Volunteer Queen to have too much going on in your life. You just need kids, the lure of school flyers, and enough money in the checking account, and you, too, can end up with one very full calendar.

"Did you sign Nick up for soccer?" my nine-year-old neighbor asked me one morning at the school bus stop.

"Yes, but I'm only coaching one team this fall," I answered.

He furrowed his brow. "No, I mean the soccer at the high school. This summer?" he explained. "I'm doing it."

There's so much soccer—and baseball and religion camp and art classes and science camp—around here, it's hard to keep track of it all. If I wanted to, I could sign my boys up for travel soccer, which meets year-round; a half-day summer soccer program sponsored by former pro player Tab Ramos; indoor soccer programs with coaches who have exotic foreign accents and rock-hard calves; and the high school program my neighbor mentioned.

That's a whole lotta soccer. And it's too much—both for my boys and for me, even when I'm not coaching. Yet it's easy to get sucked into the activity vortex when there's so much to get sucked into. All it takes is a flyer and some gossip.

First, a flyer touting art classes for kids comes home from school or in the mail. Classes will be held on Saturdays for eight weeks. *Hmmm,* you think. *He's not signed up for anything then. I'd have to drop him off at the classes two towns over after my other son's basketball games, and, on certain weekends, before a birthday party. I might have time to run to Wal-Mart and fill up my gas tank before I have to pick him up again, before rushing back home for my daughter's cheerleading practice. I could do it!*

You mention the classes to your son, who spends most evenings drawing in his room, and he shrugs. Not exactly the animated response you thought you'd get, so you put aside the flyer.

But then a friend whose child also likes to draw asks, "Did you see the flyer about the art classes?" You nod. She says, "Those classes sure helped Samantha draw better. Is Michael going to take them?" The implication of which is, "Aren't you going to give your talented child every shot he has at succeeding? I do."

You start to wonder if you've been adequately cultivating his talent. You think about the few solidly mediocre projects he's done in art class at school, and start to panic. Maybe you're not doing enough! Maybe he really needs those art classes now or else he'll never get into the Rhode Island School of Design or land that dream job with Marvel Comics, and it'll be all your fault because you didn't bring him to art class when he was nine. How could you?

Or maybe he wants to study computers, anyhow. It's hard to know nine years before college starts. Is there a computer class for kids his age? Of course there is. Maybe you need to sign him up for that one, too. How will he do it all? How will you?

The flyers and the neighbors are luring you into filling your calendar with every opportunity that comes your child's way. But while you're plowing through a snowstorm to get to art class, ask yourself: Is this the full life you've always wanted? Or is it just a full schedule?

Overscheduled Kids Don't Know How to Entertain Themselves

Maybe you're lucky enough to have a twelve-year-old trumpet aficionado who impresses family members at every holiday gathering with his rendition of *Ave Maria.* But will he dump his horn for his first taste of unscheduled freedom at the frat house anyhow? All those lessons, all that time on the road bringing him to classes and watching him play in the band at Friday night football games in the freezing rain, and he may simply give it all up the moment he gets a little free time and a foosball table.

There are lots of reasons that today's kids often have no clue how to amuse themselves. One of the most insidious is overscheduling. At my house, I can tell the overscheduled kids from the others. They stand in the middle of our garage filled with baseballs, skateboards, wagons, soccer balls, driveway chalk, and bicycles, and look at me with the kind of anticipation usually reserved for a summer camp director or whoever's in charge of March Madness. God forbid they study an ant hole for fifteen minutes. That's not on their schedule.

These kids have never had a day to just play, what with all the classes and practices and activities. When they have downtime, (meaning, they don't have to be anywhere for at least an hour), they fill it with guitar practice, homework, or staying out of Mom's hair by playing FIFA World Cup Soccer on Xbox. You know, so they can work on their defensive strategies for their travel soccer team. And their recreation soccer team. And their school soccer team.

More often than not, they eat dinner in the car en route to the next activity or alone at the kitchen table while doing their homework at 9 p.m. Every day after school, they have activities lined up, none of them involving selling lemonade at the end of the driveway or riding their bikes down to the pond to catch and release frogs. Not when there's karate and flute and gymnastics and T-ball to get to. And that's just Monday and Tuesday.

These are the same kids who later call home three times a day from college to ask, "Should I sign up for the Kant lecture series?" and "Which homework should I tackle first, Shakespeare or Psych 101?" They're lost without a Mom-driven busy, busy, busy schedule.

How will they fill their own kids' schedules when they don't even know how to manage theirs? Um, hello, Grandma?

12 Signs You've Got Too Much on Your Plate

1. You've filled up your to-do list for the week, and it's only Tuesday.
2. You dumped your child's birthday present onto the floor so you could use the Winnie the Pooh gift bag for your parents' anniversary present.
3. You keep telling yourself that your daughter's pants are Capris, when really, she outgrew them months ago.
4. You have more food stashed in your car than in your pantry.
5. You know exactly how many minutes it takes to get from the grammar school to the lacrosse field behind the municipal building if the light in between is green. Also, if it's red.
6. You haven't yet watched the season finale of your favorite TV show—the one you recorded six months ago.
7. The only time you get to sit down is in your car and in the waiting area at the Kumon tutoring center.
8. The folks at the Burger King drive-through know that you don't want pickles on your Whopper Junior before you even order it.
9. You keep extra shin guards, socks, water bottles, hockey sticks, baseballs, guitar picks, karate belts, ballet slippers, and mouth guards in your car, just in case.
10. You get all of your news on the sidelines of various youth sporting events.
11. Your PDA keeps warning you that you've got several things scheduled at once.
12. Your kids tuck you in at night.

Playtime Is Dead

Maybe you think you're doing your children a disservice by letting them play in a pile of leaves while you read *Real Simple* magazine. After all, you should be looking for teachable moments in your yard. (Photosynthesis, perhaps?) That is your job. You're a twenty-first-century parent.

As a result, playtime is dead. What else could explain the stupefying success of *The Dangerous Book for Boys*, a bestselling tome written to "recapture lazy Sunday afternoons and long summer days"? Today's kids don't have lazy Sunday afternoons and long summer days. They have swim stroke clinic and music class in Spanish. (dos classes in one! Muy bueno!) So they need a book to teach them how to skim stones, build a tree house, and fashion a slingshot from rubber bands.

Parents love this book because it reminds them of their underscheduled childhood, back before the advent of $200-an-hour college admissions counselors and cooking classes for eighteen-month-olds. Whether our generation of parents killed playtime or it was already on life support by the time we had kids, I'm not sure. Considering several towns have instituted homework- and sports-free "Family Game Nights," designed to give parents a shot at just playing with their kids, I'd say we certainly helped pull the plug. After all, we have to *schedule* playtime onto our calendars.

What's more, we have to schedule it together for that coveted quality time that eludes so many families these days. I don't ever remember my mother organizing game nights. If we wanted to play Clue, we knew where to find it in the hutch behind the blue chair, next to the Partridge Family record. My brother and I certainly didn't expect Mom to play with us, and frankly, since my brother could beat her at Pong—using his *foot*—we usually kept the game playing to ourselves.

But today's parents are supposed to play with our children, preferably with a top-rated educational toy that will teach the kids spelling, math, or geography while we sit there all smug, knowing we're making memories like we're supposed to, yet also preparing them for the SATs at the same time. God forbid we hand them a board game and leave the room. How will they learn? How would we bond?

Jen's Tips for Lightening Up Your Schedule a Bit
Act Like a Cat—Don't Come Running When People Call You

When one grandmother, who was filling in for her vacationing daughter and son-in-law, called me one night to find out what time her grandson's soccer practice was, I didn't return her call. Why? Because *I wasn't his soccer coach.* I had no idea when or where his practice was; it wasn't listed on my team's schedule. She knew I wasn't his coach, and yet, she picked me as her own personal 411.

If I had returned her call to suggest that she call her grandson's coach or the recreation department like she should have in the first place, I'd only invest my time in something that wasn't mine to begin with. Then I'd have to dig up those numbers for her, and perhaps the numbers of parents whose kids were on her grandson's team. And by the time the call was over, no doubt I'd wind up driving him to his practice, perhaps supplying shin guards and a water bottle for the kid, too. That's how it works. That's why they call me.

I inherited this burden from my mother. We call her 1-800-ROBERTA, because so many people call her for all sorts of local information. When she was at the pinnacle of her mothering career, neighbors called her about everything from which day is bulk garbage day in town to what the phone number is for the local ice skating rink. Most of the time, she had the answer. And if she didn't, she'd find it.

If she was 1-800-ROBERTA, then I was becoming www.AskJen.org. One day, the nanny for a family down the street called me to see if I knew anyone who was looking for help with childcare. "You know everyone in this neighborhood," she explained. And she was right. I hooked her up with another family that needed a nanny.

While I enjoy helping out when I can, it can get taxing. Like when I'm rushing to get my kids out the door, and some lady wants to know when her grandson's soccer practice is. So when I started being a little less available for the extraneous people, the people who don't return the favor and do seem to think my minivan is a taxi, I found that my to-do list got lighter and lighter. And so did the weight on my shoulders.

Resist the urge to help everyone out, and people will eventually stop calling you with their little time-suckers. Then you can concentrate your time on your family.

Don't Be a Frequent Flyer

You wouldn't pile everything from a Chinese food buffet onto your plate, would you? Unless you're treating the high school boys' basketball team to dinner, you couldn't possibly eat General Tso's Chicken, Mo Shu Pork, Steak Kew, and Shrimp Szechuan all in one sitting. The same goes for all those flyers and announcements for activities your kids can join. You just have to pick one or two that will fill you—and your calendar—up.

I like to plan activities that both of my boys can do at the same time. They play on the same soccer team, attend the same Cub Scouts pack meetings, race on the same swim team, and have back-to-back piano lessons on Tuesdays. That way, I'm not racing from one field or meeting or class to another.

I also try to space out activities using the holes in my boys' calendars. When Cub Scouts winds down in early June, I add a few tennis lessons on the final days of school when they have Spring Fever and could use an hour of running around the court swatting at balls with their rackets (rather than at each other with toy swords in my living room). After their swim team takes their last laps for the summer in mid-August, I schedule nothing, nada, zippo for the remaining weeks of summer. We can all use the downtime. I use mine to recycle the onslaught of flyers that arrive just before school starts in September.

Put Down the Educational Toys and Put Your Hands Where I Can See Them

Your child does not have to create a replica of the Washington Monument out of sugar cubes to make her playtime worthwhile. Nor does she have to learn how to conjugate French verbs, identify the Yangtze River on an unlabeled map, or understand the four stages of a butterfly's growth, either. Sometimes she can spend her play time simply putting pebbles in a bucket and talking to spiders. And guess what? She won't grow up to be the Village Idiot.

Back in the day (before *Baby Einstein* came along and ruined it all), my brother and our cousins and I played outside all day long in the summer. My mother didn't orchestrate our activities, except to tell us to stop hitting balls against the garage door. (Gee, our grandmother next door never told us to stop. Maybe she just couldn't hear it.)

One afternoon, my cousins and I drew roads, stores, and houses in chalk on their driveway and spent the afternoon playing in our new homemade town. It was Sim City circa 1978, and we came up with it all on our own simply because we had the freedom to play. Also, because our mothers wouldn't let us in the house.

Of course, we also spent our summer days riding our bikes into the swimming pool when my father wasn't around to wonder what bike grease does to the pool filter, and chasing after my cousin's dog, who liked to run off with our soccer ball in her mouth.

I consider these activities as much college prep as homework was. We learned things not taught at school, including how to organize ourselves, how to get along without adult supervision, how to entertain ourselves, and how to high-tail it across the yard while someone's chasing you, which, believe me, comes in handy at some collegiate gatherings.

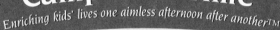

Camp Free Time

Enriching kids' lives one aimless afternoon after another™

Want to give your kids the very best there is this summer?
Sign them up for fun-in-the-sun at Camp Free Time. At Camp Free Time, we believe that
children have the innate ability to entertain themselves if the adults in their lives would just
step back and let them find out for themselves why you can't skim a three-pound rock
across a pond. Here's what we have to offer:

Pick-Up Ball

We leave out baseballs, bats, and bases and kids figure out what to do with them—without
supervision! Same goes for basketballs, tennis rackets and even volleyballs. And if the kids
have a disagreement, they actually work it out themselves.

Tree Fort

Kids play in a tree fort. That's pretty much it, but it takes up an entire afternoon.
Frankly, we're baffled by it, too.

Free Swim

Here, kids incorporate what they've learned in months of swim lessons at home.
Or, they just play Marco Polo and then have chicken fights.

Water Balloon Fight

The bigger kids fill balloons with water and tie them, and then they all toss them at each
other. Amazingly, nobody has filed a lawsuit to date.

Arts & Crafts

Campers make things without the aid of a computer. They glue leaves on Popsicle sticks and
make jewelry from beads. Do they learn about Native American cultures or discuss the rules
of nature? No, they just make stuff for Mom for the heck of it.

Lemonade Stand

Kids make lukewarm lemonade and sell it for fifty cents a Dixie cup to passers-by. Then they
take their cash and buy Webkinz cards and gum. They dump the leftover lemonade in the
shrubs and go play pick-up ball.

Camp Free Time
Enriching kids' lives one aimless afternoon after another™
1–800–KID–CAMP

Camp Free Time
Enriching kids' lives one aimless afternoon after another™
1–800–KID–CAMP

Camp Free Time
Enriching kids' lives one aimless afternoon after another™
1–800–KID–CAMP

Camp Free Time
Enriching kids' lives one aimless afternoon after another™
1–800–KID–CAMP

Camp Free Time
Enriching kids' lives one aimless afternoon after another™
1–800–KID–CAMP

Camp Free Time
Enriching kids' lives one aimless afternoon after another™
1–800–KID–CAMP

Camp Free Time
Enriching kids' lives one aimless afternoon after another™
1–800–KID–CAMP

Camp Free Time
Enriching kids' lives one aimless afternoon after another™
1–800–KID–CAMP

Camp Free Time
Enriching kids' lives one aimless afternoon after another™
1–800–KID–CAMP

SECRET SEVEN

Don't Let the Youth Sports Cartel Run Your Life

Every spring, my neighbor asks me the same question: "Are your boys going to play soccer in the fall?" She knows the answer already, the same answer it's been since kindergarten: They're going to play on the town recreation team, and I'm going to be their coach. But that's not what she's *really* asking. She's fishing to see if my younger son will join her son's travel soccer team, which has been playing together since first grade.

Usually, I dance around the answer, but this year, I stopped the sidestepping. "They're not allowed to play travel until fifth grade," I explained.

"Well why not?" she asked.

"Because it's all way too much, way too young, that's why."

She looked at me as though I'd just blasphemed the Pope through a bullhorn in St. Peter's Square.

I refused to back down. *That's right,* my stare said. *I, Jen Singer, former college soccer player, just dissed travel soccer.*

I don't know how youth sports went from the fun, easygoing games of my childhood to the win-at-any-cost, play-year-round, travel-across-the-state, you're-stuck-at-right fullback-forever-even-though-you're-only-eight cartel that it is today, but I hate it. I think it has all but ruined youth sports.

Less Is More, and More Is Going to Drive Many Kids to Quit

My mother practically came out of the womb shouting, "Give me the ball!" She loved playing ball so much, she was annoyed when her engagement ring got caught in her mitt at her company's softball games. In high school, she played basketball (half-court—this was the fifties, the poor dears), and couldn't understand why my grandfather told her she couldn't play touch football with the boys anymore when she turned sixteen.

Luckily, girls' sports changed a lot by the time Title IX landed me a spot on one of the town's recreation baseball teams, the only kid on my team with ponytails coming out from under her hat. My town started a girls' soccer league when I was nine, so I didn't have to play on the boys' team. And, unlike my mother, I got to play full-court basketball in junior high school.

Throughout my youth sports years, I was encouraged to play different positions and play many different sports—and not all in the same season. When I was invited to play on a travel soccer team at age twelve, my mom and I turned down the offer, later choosing instead to play on the county select team in high school because it required less travel and more soccer. I could choose a less intense soccer schedule and still get to play.

By the time my kids took up soccer, though, things had changed. They started Kiddie Soccer at the tender age of four, mostly because it gave me a half-hour to sit and talk to grown-ups, but also because everyone else was doing it. I coached their coed kindergarten clinics, designed to give kids some basic skills.

But one mother took issue with my coaching style on the first day of practice. When several kids were sitting down after being tagged out in a game of "Sharks and Minnows," she approached me and said, "In third-grade soccer, we don't let the kids sit down like that." She informed me, "They should be passing balls back and forth while they wait."

I pointed out that this wasn't third grade. "These kids are *five*," I said. "Some of them touched a ball for the first time this morning." I refused to get sucked into the crazy competitive world of youth sports when the kids on my team were still having Circle Time at school. I noticed she sent her husband to practice after that.

It pains me that there are kids in my town who are stuck playing positions they don't like because their coaches won't let them try something new. There are eight-year-olds who are playing three sports in one season—heck, in one weekend, every weekend. There are ten-year-olds who are doing homework in their mothers' cars while they race to another game halfway across the state. And there are plenty of twelve-year-olds who quit their favorite sport because it wasn't fun anymore.

Less is more, and more is way too much, way too young.

Mother's Day Has Been Canceled

Several of my neighbors spent their most recent Mother's Day on the sidelines of a soccer field forty-five minutes from home. One of my neighbors, who had just had a baby two weeks earlier, was less than thrilled that her son and her husband would be spending Mother's Day not with her and the baby, but with a bunch of other eight-year-olds and their families who had all been hijacked for the afternoon.

As a coach, it would never occur to me to schedule a game on Mother's Day or Father's Day. Or to send a couple of seven-year-olds to a weekend soccer tournament an hour down the turnpike on Fourth of July weekend. As a player, I would have quit soccer long before college if I had to play four three-on-three soccer games on a ninety-degree hazy, hot, and humid Saturday while my friends were home, splashing in the community lake and eating bomb pops. When will kids get to be kids?

In today's youth sports, there's little room for family time, unless it's spent on the sidelines or in the stands. There's always another tournament or a "big game" or a much-needed practice to interfere with a family trip to Disney or Grandma's seventy-fifth birthday party.

If you're in the state championships or being scouted by college recruiters, maybe Grandma will understand. But the rest of the games? Are they really that important? I don't think so, but I seem to have little company here. Youth sports has weeded out anybody but the die-hards, and at a very young age.

It's doubtful that your kid's U-9 baseball team's game against the town's rival will land your child the college scholarship you dream of. And if it did, would the scholarship money even come close to covering the money you've spent on new cleats and helmets each season, catcher's gear, registration fees, private coaching, and gas? Probably not.

But parents are afraid to speak up about their kids' crazy sports schedules, because they don't want to risk retaliation by the coach. The kid who comes to every practice and game, never once complaining about playing a position she hates, gets rewarded with playing time. The kid whose parents suggest that perhaps the team doesn't need a practice on Sunday when they just had a game (which they won) on Saturday night, will probably warm the bench.

And so parents find themselves tag-teaming to get one kid to her swim tournament and another to his lacrosse game (after baseball, of course), wondering where their weekend went. And their Mother's Day. And Father's Day. And their family time.

10 Signs Your Family Is in Too Deep with Youth Sports

1. Your child is signing and selling his Little League baseball cards on the school bus—and there's actually a market for them. (Hello, eBay?)
2. You get in the car to drive to work and instead wind up at a soccer field thirty miles away, wondering where everyone is.
3. Your youngest's first words were "FOUL BALL!"
4. The pizza delivery guy can spot you on the sidelines out of a group of forty or so parents.
5. You can guide customers to the right section in Sports Authority better than the salespeople can.
6. When you hear the referee blow the end-of-game whistle on ESPN, you reflexively start packing sporting gear into a duffel bag, shouting, "C'mon! We've got to get to the lacrosse game now!"
7. You own the most tricked-out beach chairs in the neighborhood, complete with not one, but two cup holders, a built-in umbrella, and an adjustable foot rest, and yet you never have time to go to the beach.
8. You've got a professional-grade batting cage and pitching machine in your front yard, but you don't have enough money to fix your leaking bathtub.
9. On game days, your minivan gets more miles on it than a limo on prom night.
10. The two most relaxing words in your vocabulary are "home game."

There's No Room for Late Bloomers

Every spring, I sign up my boys for five semi-private swim lessons with a woman whose son swims in the Nationals. I tell them it's to warm them up for their swim team season, which starts when school ends. But really, it's a crash course designed to keep them from swallowing the wake of other kids who swim on competitive teams year-round.

At nine, my son was a late bloomer as far as our community's swim team goes. Unlike the other kids his age, he hadn't joined the team at age six, when, frankly, he probably would have drowned halfway across the 20-meter swim lane while I dove in fully clothed to save him. He just wasn't ready. More importantly, he wasn't interested, so I didn't push him.

Luckily, the coaches let him swim with his brother in the eight-and-under group until he felt comfortable enough to compete with the nine- and ten-year-old boys, some of whom can butterfly faster than I can swim freestyle (and they're a good foot shorter than I am).

He did just fine his first season on the team, even winning the Most Improved Swimmer. But whenever we start up our spring crash course lessons, I worry how much he missed over the winter, while the other kids spent their weekends at twelve-hour swim tournaments, and we did what? Made snow forts in the backyard.

After I took him to a New York Yankees game this spring, he announced he wanted to join the baseball team next year. That's great, except he hasn't been on an organized baseball team since kindergarten, when he spent his Saturday mornings writing his name in the dirt at his T-ball games.

Will he be able to compete with the other fourth graders who have been playing travel ball on two different teams as well as recreation baseball? Or will youth sports, which cater to the elite few, have no room for a late bloomer like him? Hopefully, it won't be painful to find out.

Jen's Rules for Staying Sane in Youth Sports
Play One Sport Per Season

Sports should be like a tasting menu for kids. Let them try a few before they specialize in one when they get older. I realize this is near impossible if they want to play on travel teams, which generally practice and play year-round. But if you stick with your town's recreation department teams and school sports, it's much easier.

My younger son, whose first word was "ball," plays soccer in the fall, basketball in the winter, baseball in the spring, and races on the swim team in the summer. His favorite sport is baseball, and he hopes to be a professional player some day. But I'm not about to ask him to give up his fall soccer fun to head down the road to the Major Leagues at the age of eight. Nor will I let him play both sports in the same season. His knees can thank me later.

Teens are getting overuse sports injuries that doctors say they used to witness in twenty-somethings just a few years ago. If you think your kid's coach or the other parents have your kid's health in mind, think again. Why else would Little League Baseball have to step in and institute a per-game pitching maximum for players as young as seven? To save their rotator cuffs from surgery at age fifteen, that's why.

Besides, though he adores baseball, he really enjoys his other sports, too. And I enjoy kicking soccer balls, shooting hoops, playing catch, and swimming with him, too. Maybe that won't help him get a spot on the New York Mets lineup fifteen years from now like he dreams of, but he'll have a fun childhood to look back on.

Just Say No to Too Much, Too Soon

Does your first grader really want to spend her weekends at twelve-hour-long swim meets? Do you? If the answer is no, why are you doing it?

Just say no to more teams, more practices, more competition, and more nights rushing to yet another game in yet another town. Just say no to eight-year-olds relegated to left field for the entire season when they really want to try shortstop. Just say no to goalie coaches and private lacrosse lessons for kids as young as six, and to 6 a.m. hockey practice before school. Just say no, and others will, too. And then you can create the kind of youth sports you remember from your childhood.

I coach boys' soccer in part because I love the sport and in part because I love the kids. But I admit I also coach so that I can create the kind of atmosphere I think belongs on a field with eleven second graders who all want to chase the ball in a giant mob, like a scene from *Lord of the Flies,* only without the pig heads on sticks.

I try to give the kids a chance to play several different positions so that no one gets branded as, say, left midfield, at the age of seven. I try to make practices fun, even chasing them up and down the field, or popping a high ball over their heads and into the goal just to show them what a girl can do. And I encourage them to learn from their mistakes and move on.

Over the years, I've earned a bit of a reputation in recreation soccer. At the end of last season, several fathers—whose kids played on opposing teams—offered to be my assistant coach next season, so that their sons could play on my team.

I am greatly flattered, and also realistic: I'd never make it as a travel soccer coach. My philosophy on youth soccer would be crushed by the men—and it's almost exclusively men—who run other teams to win at all costs. If you want your kid to spend his weekends learning how to elbow the opposing team without getting caught by the ref, I'm not the coach for the job. If you want your kid to have fun while learning, drop by my recreation soccer practice next fall.

I've learned to say yes to less. And so far, my kids and the boys on my soccer teams are loving every minute of it, even overtime in the freezing rain.

Think Long-Term, Act Short-Term

There was a boy on my first- and second-grade recreation soccer team who clearly did not want to be there. I'd put him in at right halfback, and he'd wander around the field as though I'd just dropped him off in the middle of Stuttgart without a map or any workable knowledge of German. The poor kid was lost.

His parents kept bringing him back to practices and to games, but it didn't get any better. I tried to pull him aside and explain the basics of soccer to him, but he just stared at me blankly. When he didn't show up for our third game, I called his mom, who's a friend of mine.

"He doesn't even want to put on his cleats," she said. "I don't know what to do."

"He's seven," I answered. "If he doesn't want to play soccer, don't make him."

She sounded relieved, as though she needed my approval to let her son quit soccer. Normally, I adhere to the rule my mother enforced when my brother and I were kids: Finish what you start. But back then, we were finishing seventh-grade basketball. We weren't decked out in shin guards and thrown onto a field where we didn't want to be when we were just in first grade.

Maybe her son will be like my son was when it came to T-ball. Someday, he'll go to a Major League Soccer game and decide he wants to take up the sport at the age of ten. Or maybe he'll take up the piano. Who knows? But if he's just not that into it when he's still little enough to want to spend his Saturday mornings sipping juice boxes and watching *Clifford the Big Red Dog*, let him stay home.

If you push him into it now, he'll really hate the sport later when he's mature enough to truly enjoy it. And then you'll miss your youth sports window, leaving you with an eleven-year-old who wants to spend his Saturday mornings sipping Jolt and playing *Pirates of the Caribbean* on Xbox.

The Road to the College Sports Scholarship

Two Years Old: Uncle Joe notices that little Jake has a heck of an arm for a toddler. Spends much of the family vacation teaching Jake to throw a wiffle ball in his general direction without knocking over his beer.

Three Years Old: Mom signs Jake up for Throw-and-Go classes, where toddlers are encouraged to throw foam balls and run around bases in 1-2-3 order. (Jake likes to skip first base, worrying Mom that perhaps he's not cut out for baseball.)

Four Years Old: Dad persuades the town's Recreation Commissioner to allow Jake to join T-ball, even though he's technically five months too young. Jake scores his first home run, largely because the shortstop was busy drawing in the sand and the catcher's mask was so oversized he couldn't see the ball to pick it up. Dad starts dreaming of baseball scouts.

Six Years Old: Dad decides that Jake isn't learning enough on the Recreation Team and signs him up for a traveling team. As a result, Mom puts more than a thousand miles on her minivan this season.

Eight Years Old: Mom and Dad make Jake quit soccer, a sport he's not as good at but enjoys because his friends are on his team, so Jake can focus better on baseball, which has now become a year-round sport for him, even though they live in snow country.

Nine Years Old: The family moves to Florida, where kids play baseball outdoors year-round, to give Jake a leg-up on the college competition. After all, they have only nine more years until college. Heartbroken, his little sister gives up skiing. She overhears Mom say, "She wasn't competing at the top level anyhow," and decides to bury herself in Harry Potter books and bags of Cheetos.

Ten Years Old: Mom enrolls Jake in a training center for child athletes. While Jake's new school buddies spend their afternoons reenacting *Star Wars*, Jake is trying to run while pulling weights behind him, as an instructor yells, "C'mon! You don't want it enough! Pull!"

Twelve Years Old: Worried that Jake is losing his competitive edge, Mom and Dad send Jake to a sports psychologist, who helps him "see the ball coming off his fingertips and past the batter." Also, she helps him deal with the side effects of puberty, which are taking his "eye off the prize," as Dad puts it, and onto Jessica McCloskey, who sits next to him in Spanish class.

Fourteen Years Old: Jake is the starting pitcher on his high school's JV team and his traveling team. New Little League Baseball rules prevent him from throwing more than seventy-five pitches per game, but lucky for him, his traveling team doesn't follow Little League Baseball rules.

Sixteen Years Old: Jake hears a loud "pop" while pitching. Looks like his arm has what's called a "sports overuse injury," and it's just months until college recruiters start to scout! Jake has surgery, and his arm heals just in time for the spring season. Meanwhile, Mom gives him a kit designed to teach him how to snag a college scholarship.

Seventeen Years Old: Two colleges offer Jake partial scholarships. He takes the best offer: $2,000 a year for a small college in the Pacific Northwest. That's $8,000 total, or about $10,000 less than Mom and Dad have spent on his youth baseball career. And then there's the cost of flights to go see his college games. But don't worry, Mom and Dad. When Jake graduates, he'll have a degree in accounting. Maybe he can help lower your tax burden or at least loan you a few bucks.

Thirty Years Old: Jake comes home from work, plops on the couch, exhausted from the long hours of tax season. He asks Jake Jr., now eighteen months, to throw him a ball, and wouldn't you know it, he gets it right to Daddy! He's a chip off the old block. Jake Sr. smells a scholarship in the making.

PART TWO

Slacker Mom Isn't as Cool as She Appears to Be

Do you really aspire to be the mom who serves cocktails at playdates and thinks being called a "MILF" by drunken twenty-somethings at the Applebee's bar is a wonderful compliment?

SECRET EIGHT

Your Kid Shouldn't Be Wearing a T-shirt That Reads "Future Trophy Wife"

I have a confession to make: I once came home from college wearing a Boston University T-shirt with a drawing of my school's mascot, a smirking-but-otherwise-not-doing-anything-nasty Rhett the Terrier, that read, "Do It Doggie Style." When I saw the look on my father's face, I realized I had made a mistake. He looked like he might melt into the floor like the Wicked Witch of the West. Poor guy. I never wore the shirt again, even at school.

So, what's the difference between that moronic shirt and, say, a modern "I Take Candy from Strangers" top? When I wore my tasteless T-shirt, I was twenty—an adult, even if I wasn't dressing like one. These days, though, kids as young as ten are wearing offensive, if not stomach-turning, T-shirts that often-times their parents even *buy for them* at stores popular with tweens like Hot Topic, Abercrombie and Fitch, Target, and even Limited Too.

To me, that's just one small step away from the lifestyle of a girl I went to summer camp with back in the day, whose psychologist parents thought it wise to purchase and smoke pot with their kids, so they could "experiment in a controlled atmosphere."

Certainly, there's got to be a T-shirt for that. Maybe a picture of a gingerbread man cookie toking a doobie with the words "I (got) baked with my mom last night."

When your kids wear obscene T-shirts, you're not supposed to giggle. You're supposed to gasp and start melting into the ground like my father nearly did. And you are most certainly *not* supposed to actually supply your fifteen-year-old daughter with a "Dirty. Blonde." shirt.

Your job is to confiscate said shirt, and burn it in the fireplace along with your son's "Tell your boobs to stop staring at my eyes" sweatshirt and the bumper sticker from his bedroom door that reads, "Dip me in honey and throw me to the women." And then you're supposed to ground everybody while mumbling, "My father would have sent me to Parris Island if I had worn that thing in his house!" before wandering off to watch CNN and sulk.

We're all going to hell in a handbasket, and our children's clothes are leading the way. It seems that the raunchier our stuff gets, the more we welcome it by loosening our grip on decency. When half the toddlers at your playgroup are wearing T-shirts that read, "Don't look at me. That smell is coming from Grandpa," how long will it be before their attitudes match their outfits?

Raunch for Sale

Sadly, the T-shirts we used to sneak peeks at in Spencer Gifts, the ever-cheesy tchotchke store, are now practically everywhere, and today they're way worse. Take, for example, the eyeful my kids and I get when we take our annual trip to the boardwalk in Wildwood, New Jersey. En route to the arcade games (where we spend upwards of forty bucks on games that net them two-dollar stuffed animals and a handful of Chinese handcuffs), we are assaulted by the raunchy T-shirts for sale at boardwalk shops, not to mention on teens and—sheesh!—even tweens who pass by.

My boys see T-shirts (in baby and toddler sizes, no less) that read, "I'm a sucker for boobs," and "Bozo the Clown can kiss my ass. Get me a stripper." Mmmmmm. Classy. Would little Tommy like a juice box? Or maybe a Heineken?

When did we go from buying our nephews cute little shirts that say, "Two's aren't terrible . . . I'm having a great time!" to toddler tees that read, "Hung like a five-year-old"? I imagine it was sometime right after Ozzie Osbourne got his own reality show and Madonna started writing children's books.

I hate to say "when I was a kid," but, when I was a kid, our most provocative T-shirts read, "I Don't Give a Damn about My Bad Reputation." We wore them at Joan Jett concerts located in areas where we feared for the safety of our cars, our leather jackets, and our little sisters. We didn't wear them to go for Chinese food with the 'rents or to the high school girls' basketball team's division championship game in the school gym.

I hate to say "kids these days," but, kids these days dress like Lindsay Lohan on a bender even when they're just heading to the library. They're not wearing Violent Femmes T-shirts to look as cool as the punk rockers at CBGB's like we did back in high school. They're wearing Mommy-bought "Rehab is for quitters" shirts to family picnics while their eight-year-old sisters are donning "Super cute babe" belly T-shirts at school.

It's no wonder our kids are donning raunchy clothes (and often, the attitude to match). Mommy and Daddy started it. Some pregnant mothers and their husbands have gone wild. Now we have maternity tees that read, "Sex ed dropout," "Contraception malfunction," and "Knocked up"—and that's got nothing to do with the movie. Do the ladies in the waiting room at your OB/GYN chuckle when you wear that? Or do they move to a different couch and pretend to be engrossed in a seven-month-old issue of *Better Homes & Gardens?*

Worse are the tees for the proud fathers-to-be, such as the drawing of a man next to a pregnant woman with the word "Bullseye" above it. Please, *please* don't wear that when you announce your good news to your parents. And find something else to put on when you go to your baby shower, because the "He shoots . . . he scores!" shirt with a drawing of sperm playing hockey on it simply doesn't belong in the same room as a "Welcome Baby" sign adorned with little pink teddy bears.

Playgroup or Happy Hour?

If the babies and toddlers at your playgroup wear these tees, it's time to switch playgrounds:

- All Mommy wanted was a backrub
- I drink 'til I pass out. Just like my Daddy.
- I'm what happened in Vegas.
- My mom puts out.
- I'm a boob man.
- Playground pimp.
- Put down the cake. This is my first one and you look like you've had plenty.
- They spank me and I like it.

For Adult Use

Someone surely must have bought the Peekaboo Pole Dancing kit that was for sale, however briefly, in the toy section of the website for Tesco, Britain's version of Target. Parents shopping for Christmas presents stumbled upon the kit, which includes an extendable chrome pole, "sexy garter," instructional DVD, and "100

Peekaboo Dance Dollars," which I guess is like Monopoly money for women who like to wear G-strings in their living rooms.

But wait! There's more! You could also purchase a strip poker game called "Peekaboo Poker," plus T-shirts—and even thongs—for girls as young as six with the slogan, "So many boys, so little time."

Mortified parents managed to get Tesco to take some of the offensive items down from the site, even though the company claimed the pole dancing kit was clearly marked "For Adult Use" and—this is amazing—denied the kit was sexually oriented. I guess you're supposed to put the garter on the end of the pole and dust your blinds with it, like a pink and black lace Swiffer.

But as T-shirts—and America—get racier, it gets easier to lose sight of what should be acceptable. After all, we went from watching "Family Hour" TV between 7 and 9 p.m. to today's broadcast of *Girls Next Door,* the so-called reality show about the exploits of Hugh Hefner's top-three scantily clad girlfriends. (Only a thirteen-year-old boy could believe that's reality.)

The show airs not on the Playboy Channel, but on *E!* where, presumably, your daughter goes to find out the latest news on her crush, Orlando Bloom. Is the show on at 10 p.m.? Nah. Saturday at 4 p.m. Maybe your kid will finish her soccer game in time to get home to see it. Then you can drop by the Playboy store and get her a *Girls Next Door* T that apparently has just enough room for a pair of double D's. While you're there, you might as well get your daughter the "Uh-ohhhh. Somebunny's gonna get it" shirt.

And then there's the reason I'm frequently grateful I don't have daughters: Bratz dolls. Made for girls who aren't quite ready for training bras, the outfits these dolls wear reveal more than Pamela Anderson at, well, pretty much anywhere she goes. If your daughter shares their "passion for fashion," you can drop by Macy's or Dillards for their very own Lil Bratz couture. Lucky you.

7 Signs Your Kids Are Up to No Good

1. Your jewelry box is missing—and so is the shovel.
2. There's a trail of broccoli leading to the bathroom door.
3. You just heard "ribbit" coming from the bird cage.
4. Your TiVo disk is filled with nothing but *Jimmy Neutron* episodes.
5. Your son, who's surfing eBay, wants to know if twenty bucks is a good price for string instruments. And he's taking pictures of his violin.
6. Your couch cushions crunch when you sit on them.
7. Your neighbor called to tell you that the bright-colored magnetic letters on her fridge now spell "MILF"—and that your kids are on their way home.

Can I Put a V-Chip on Your Shirt?

Here are some of the clothes you can find for Back to School: a black messenger bag that says, "Kill from first to last," inspired by a punk band with an album entitled, *Teen Angst Has a Body Count,* and a pink shirt in junior sizes that reads, "I might like you better if you just shut up every once in a while."

So you don't shop where these items are touted for Back to School? Wise choice. Let's see what's for sale over at every teen's favorite store, Abercrombie and Fitch. There you can find men's tees that read, "My favorite number is 3: Bring a friend," "I'd do me," and "Mt. Herinback" with a drawing of a large male moose on it. (That last one took me a few minutes to sort out, so take your time. Unless you're eating. Then skip it.)

Thankfully, the kids tees at Abercrombie are nothing more than sixteen-dollar ads for their store. If you're lucky, your son won't have a big growth spurt before school starts and start shopping in the men's section. The tees for your teen daughter are tamer there, too, though I'm not sure I'd want my sixteen-year-old to wear the words, "Best you'll never have" on her chest near any group of males, especially if it's nighttime and they've scored some Miller Lite.

Over at Old Navy, your daughter can choose between the kinda cute "The dog 8 my homework" and the kinda dangerous "I study boys." You just know she's going to hear cat calls inviting her to "study hall."

I'm sure the "Sister for free" tee sounded cute to the people who designed it, but do you want your kid to wear that when he's accompanying his sister onto the rides at the traveling carnival? No. Especially if his sister is wearing the "free range chick" shirt. Et tu, Wal-Mart?

Over in Sears' young men's department, your son can buy a T-shirt depicting squirrels in a tree over the words, "It's all fun until someone loses a nut." And at K-Mart, girls have attitude. Thanks to their T-shirts for sale, your little sugar-and-spice can demand, "Don't just stand there. Buy me something." Or warn people, "Being cute got me this far." Or just declare herself the "Princess of Everything." My favorite? "Blame my parents." Oh, I do, honey. I do.

So, how do you let your kids stay hip without letting them cross the line into moral decay in a world where "Hang up and drive, jackass!" bumper stickers are pasted on otherwise family-friendly minivans?

Jen's Tips for Letting the Kids Express Themselves without Sounding Like a Character on South Park

Take the Grandma Test

If you wouldn't let your kid go to dinner at Grandma's in her "Stop staring. They don't talk." T-shirt, don't let her out of the house in it, either. If Grandma isn't exactly the arbiter of good taste, pick someone else. If she got invited to a picnic with, say, Condoleezza Rice, would you let her wear a tee declaring, "I taught your boyfriend that thing you like."

You might think, "Well, she's just going to the mall with her friends." But guess who else is going to the mall tonight? The AP teacher she's been trying to persuade to write a glowing evaluation for her college applications. Is she gonna get a chuckle out of it, or will your daughter wish she had a sweater?

When she gets to college, she can buy all the stupid T-shirts she wants and wear them around campus where, presumably, her peers will find her ironic, if not downright radical, even though a dozen other women have the very same shirt, which at least one pairs with her "This is what a feminist looks like" hat for even more droll irony. Ah, college kids.

But for now, if they're going to spend any substantial time in the Land of the Grown-Ups, the obnoxious, rude, and downright offensive T-shirts don't belong. Just ask Grandma. And Condi Rice.

It's Hip to Be Square

Face it, adults love geeky kids, kids who talk—not mumble—to them. And adults—teachers, guidance counselors, coaches, and college admissions staff—hold the keys to those kids' future.

I'm not saying that your teens have to dress like the "real square cat" from the Stray Cats *Rock This Town* video, complete with bow tie and pants that come up to their chests. It's perfectly fine for teens to be fashionable around adults, just as long as "fashionable" doesn't mean they've got their thongs hanging out of their pants, like the young woman I saw on an HGTV show one weekend.

She leaned over to check out the dishwasher in the condo she was considering buying and, oh, hello, black lace thong! I switched the channel. I don't care where you live, sweetheart, as long as I don't have to see that again. If you let your teen dress that way now, she, too, might wind up househunting with her underwear hanging out. Or attending Thanksgiving dinner at the home of her new fiancé's parents. Good to meet you, Victoria's Secret!

Go ahead and let your teens wear jeans with holes in them and Hollister hoodies. As long as they're not going to a job interview, that's fine. And tweens can drop by Limited Too to pick up some cute tees, matching pedal pushers, and some "low-rise lace and rhinestone panties" that no one will see anyhow.

But wearing a "Keep your hands to myself" tee to go pick up a date isn't going to win your son any points with his would-be girlfriend's father. Point out to him that in order to earn trust with adults who are the gatekeepers to what he wants, including girlfriends, jobs, cars, and letters of recommendation, he's not going to get it as easily (or, perhaps at all) with an "I'm not drunk, I'm just a bad driver" bumper sticker on his car.

What about younger kids? Well, who are you going to trust to hang out with your daughter? The girl who wears the "Cheer! Cheer! Cheer!" T-shirt when she comes over for a sleep-over? Or the girl who's wearing the "Bet you wish your girlfriend was hot like me" belly shirt? Personally, I'd check the latter's bag for contraband or find an excuse to send her home, but then, I'm the mother of boys.

The "Lock up your daughters" T-shirt might look cute on your toddler, but consider your relatives when you head down that slippery slope. Will Uncle Joey see that as an invitation to get his nephew his own "funny" apparel, and if so, do you really want your son to wear an "I get boob whenever I want (and Daddy's jealous)" sweatshirt to your La Leche meeting? Or will that make you feel like a boob?

When it comes to clothes, it's hip to be square whether you're two or twenty-two. Save the "If you think I'm a bitch, you should meet my mother" for, oh, I dunno, Paris Hilton's baby shower.

Kids Aren't Mini-adults

Even though they make *Playboy* T-shirts in a size 6X, it doesn't mean your kid should wear it. And even though animated characters in PG-rated movies nowadays say "crap" (sigh), it doesn't mean your kid should display the word on his clothing, no matter how funny his Uncle Joey thinks it is. Just because they make certain clothes for tots doesn't mean that your tots should wear them—and I don't just mean the obviously obnoxious clothes, either. Your child is not a miniature version of you.

If you put her in a "Princess" T-shirt, she's going to believe that you think she should be treated like royalty. And if you buy your son the "How to stay out of trouble: Don't do anything wrong. Don't get caught. Blame your friend." tee from Target, you're giving him permission to weasel out of getting in trouble by pinning the blame on his buddies. At the very least, you're acknowledging that he's a troublemaker and saying that's fine with you.

The "Class is now in session" tee with the drawing of the soccer ball is cute. The "Your lips are moving, but all I hear is blah, blah, blah" is not so cute, especially when he's sent to the principal's office. The "So many boys, so little time" T-shirt is stomach turning, frankly. Save it for your first night out after your divorce, because it doesn't belong on your second-grade girl.

We are supposed to protect our children from mature themes, though I'm not exactly sure what's mature about a "Jesus loves you, but everyone else thinks you're an asshole" bumper sticker. Sometimes I wish that people and their cars had V-chips like my TV does, but at least I can keep the crap off my kid's backs—until they go to college and get their own stupid T-shirts, just like their mother did back in the day.

10 Things to Teach Your Daughters

1. Never get your eyebrows waxed by a woman who draws hers on.
2. Cute shoes can be like St. Bernard puppies: adorable at first, but rather cumbersome later.
3. Never ask a man what's he's thinking, because chances are, it has to do with bacon double cheeseburgers or *MythBusters*—and not you.
4. The women you read about in history books—the true role models—wore underpants in public.
5. You can wear cleats and pumps in the same day, and look great in both.
6. Stoves, dishwashers, vacuums, and other such appliances are gender-neutral.
7. Diamonds are a girl's best friend, but a cat is nicer to curl up with at night.
8. If someone says, "You throw like a girl," reply, "Thank you!"
9. The stomach flu is not a diet plan—but it sure is a great head start.
10. Try to picture what that tattoo would look like on Grandma's breast before you get one that will last the rest of your life.

SECRET NINE

Don't Wait on Daddy Like He's a Houseguest

My husband must think the kitchen chairs are chilly. That's got to be the reason he drapes his coat on them when he comes home from work at night. Naturally, this drives me crazy, because (a) I have to look at his big ol' coat all evening long while I'm trying to concentrate on *Law & Order* in the adjoining family room, and (b) the closet is just five feet from the kitchen table.

Granted, our closet was built in 1970 when, apparently, people and their outerwear were much smaller. It's not easy stuffing a twenty-first-century Eddie Bauer goose-down parka with fleece lining and detachable hood with faux fur trim into a closet designed for small wool pea coats and a pair or two of Converse All-Stars.

I've grown tired of nagging him to hang up his coat. Sometimes I stuff it into the closet myself, like a frazzled air traveler trying to cram her too-big-to-be-a-carry-on bag into an overhead bin. Sometimes, I move it to another room or closet, just to watch him try to find it.

But I don't carefully put it away. Because if I start doing that, I might as well say, "You're a guest here. Let me take care of that." Soon, I'd be fixing him drinks and fetching his slippers, until one day I'd find myself vacuuming under his feet while he reads the newspaper and munches on a sandwich.

The closet might think it's still 1970, but I don't. Frankly, I don't think my husband does, either—especially since I stopped treating him like a guest in his own home.

Is He a Fabergé Egg?

My mother-in-law was very worried. My younger son had kept my husband and me up nights for months in a row, and we were exhausted. With a sleepless baby and an active toddler to care for all day—and all night—I was absolutely spent.

My mother-in-law expressed her concern: "I feel sorry for Pete. After all, at work he has to *think*."

He has to think.

Did he have to think (on about four hours of constantly inter-rupted sleep) when my toddler raced for the road while a van was speeding around the corner toward our driveway? No, that was me. Did he have to think when our toddler climbed into the sink and turned on the hot water? Nope. Me again. How about the choking hazard fished from my kid's mouth? Not him. *Me.*

When our kids were little, my husband actually had it *easier* than I did, but because what he did was called "work" and what I did was called "staying home," I guess his mother thought *he* had it rough. And sometimes, I treated him as if that were true.

Yet he went off to work where he could sit for hours and have conversations with adults and never once stick his hand down anyone's pants to see if they needed changing, or endure a temper tantrum in the middle of the supermarket over a box of sugar-coated marshmallow cereal with a picture of Buzz Lightyear on it.

In short, he had extended periods of peace, while I had a nearly around-the-clock barrage of chaos. If anyone needed my mother-in-law's concern, it was me. After all, I was the one driving her grandchildren around on the kind of sleep deprivation usually reserved for lab rats in a nervous system study.

But somewhere along the way, somebody decided that men need extra care that women don't and, even though there's far more gender equality than ever before, many moms still believe that.

That's why you see mothers rescuing their husbands from changing diapers or watching the kids—his kids, too, by the way. It's why when men clean the toilet, they're practically heroes, darn near expecting a parade down Broadway among banners that read: "One small powder room for man . . . one giant leap for mankind!" But when we do it, it goes unnoticed. It's also why my mother-in-law felt sorry for her son.

Mommy's Helper

It starts with a four-letter word: "help." You're at a jewelry party when the conversation inevitably turns to husbands. One woman complains that her husband never puts his clothes in the hamper. Another says her husband can't get their daughter ready in the morning without her ending up looking like Pippi Longstocking on a bad hair day. Another says her husband spends his entire weekend working on the lawn, even though the lawn is smaller than their living room.

You don't want to husband bash, so you offer meekly, "Well, my husband *helps*." And there it is. You're proud because an adult who lives in your house and is a parent to your children lends a helping hand now and then. If your college roommate had merely *helped*, you wouldn't have been so proud, now would you have? You'd have transferred to another dorm by October after spending a month putting her dirty underwear in the hamper and scraping her toothpaste off the sink. Well, at least she left the toilet seat down.

Whether you have a paying job or you're home with the kids all day every day, once you suggest that your husband should *help* you, you might as well give him a sticker and a lollipop for being a wonderful little aide.

Wedding Vows You Wish Your Husband Had Made

- I promise to listen to what you say past the verb and, at times, well into the paragraph.
- I vow to locate the hamper, understand its function, and use it correctly, especially after I've changed the oil in my car.
- I will buy birthday presents for my mother. And cards, too.
- I will never use the word "we're" before "pregnant."
- I will never pretend that I can't hear the kids at night. I'll even start to get out of bed long before you sigh angrily and throw the blankets off.
- I promise to finish all projects that I start, so you don't have to look at a half-painted wall or a gutter duct-taped to the roof.
- I vow to put the toilet seat down, especially late at night when you're not wearing your glasses.
- I promise never to utter the words, "Well, how much did that cost?" when you're showing off your new outfit to your mother.
- I will not act like a hero for emptying the dishwasher, making a bed, or changing a blowout diaper in a public bathroom because I'll bet you do that all the time.
- I vow to save you a piece of chocolate cake even when you say you're dieting, and then to pretend not to notice when you sneak down to eat it at midnight.

Your husband is not the Assistant to the Chief, even though it's true that he probably doesn't even begin to think of all the things you do, such as, "Are we out of milk?" "Did I sign that permission slip this morning?" and "Is that chocolate on that chair? God, I hope that's chocolate." Once you start acting like the default parent and housekeeper, he has no reason to think—or act—otherwise.

Honey? Where's the . . . ?

Ever wish your husband would learn to turn his head ever so slightly so that he could see the salad dressing in the fridge before he asks where it is? Or that he'd just go ahead and make a decision on something without conferring with you first?

I had just had surgery when my husband called on his way home from work to ask if he should pick up a pizza. I hadn't thought about dinner, nor much of anything except when I could take my next painkiller and if the family on *Trading Spaces* was really going to paint their neighbor's bedroom poo-poo brown. Still, I thought pizza was a spectacular idea.

"Okay, get a large cheese and a large mushroom," he ordered.

I tried to imagine myself asking him to order the pizza after he had surgery, but I couldn't. When he had surgery, he laid in bed for a week. Maybe it was my fault that I'd gotten dressed and moved to the couch.

"Take this down," I replied. "838-1700. That's the number for the pizza place. They'd love to hear from you." And I hung up.

Maybe that was a little—how should I say it?—bitchy of me. But really now, when he simply has the flu and not, say, major abdominal surgery, all of his responsibilities come to a screeching halt, whereas I keep on cleaning the bathroom no matter how sick I am.

Even when I'm physically down and out, I am still in charge of all sorts of things, including scheduling the kids' dentist and doctor appointments, searching the house for the empty tissue box/old sock/oatmeal container/ "silly hat"/coin collection/whatever else the teacher has requested this time, making sure my son has nice shoes and a tie for his communion, buying birthday gifts for kids we barely know, washing baseball/basketball/soccer uniforms in time for the big game, and making sure the Tooth Fairy has enough cash tonight.

And yet here I'd just had surgery—removing organs, even— and somehow, it was *my* job to order the goddamn pizza. No thanks. I'll just have a Percocet instead.

Since then, he's programmed the number for the pizza place into his cell phone's directory, though he doesn't need it. If I ask, "What's the number for the pizza place?" he can recite it like a frat house pledge rattling off the Cardinal Principles of justice, harmony, and brotherly love: "838-1700!"

In short, he gets it now.

Slacking Off

You might think that letting Hubby off the hook from all things home and childcare is actually a Super Mom trait. Picture the woman who runs her house like a cross between Martha Stewart and a West Point cadet: She wants things done right and she wants them done now, soldier.

But when you give up the ongoing battle that often comes with who-does-what around the house, you're slacking off, even if it doesn't feel like it when you're packing the kids' school lunches at midnight.

Sometimes it's just plain easier to vacuum around your husband's feet while he watches football and munches on potato chips than to ask for his help. If you've got (or trained) a spouse who thinks that real men don't clean toilets, it takes more energy to get him to stop complaining and get off his butt to help you than it does to clean the house.

But that's all part of his evil plan. When you suggest that he fold the laundry or sweep the crumbs off the kitchen floor, he grumbles and mopes until he's generally miserable to live with.

Then the next time you ask him for help, all he has to do is make that face like you've just asked if he wants a colonoscopy on the dining room table, and you give up and do all the work yourself. Like Pavlov's dog, he has trained *you*. So, how can you keep from falling into that trap?

Jen's Tips for Getting Hubby to Help Around the House
Don't Do It

My father has a magic underwear drawer. He takes out a clean pair, wears it, puts it in the hamper, and voila! A fresh pair appears in his drawer.

My husband has no such drawer. In fact, he's been doing his own laundry since he decided I might ruin his clothes with the way I do laundry. Gee, I don't know how he got this idea, but that's just fine with me.

Now, this wouldn't work with the bathrooms, the kitchen floor, or anything that requires dusting. These things are not important to him, and if I don't do them, or if I don't ask him to do them, they just don't get cleaned.

Find out what matters most to him and then don't do it.

And for Pete's sake, don't do his job for him. That's how we women end up taking on way too much—and then we complain that we have way too much to do. Everyone else seems to think that's okay. In fact, it's ingrained in our society, at least here in the suburbs, as I witnessed one September night at the boys' recreation league soccer draft, where I was the only female coach.

When we finally selected our teams, the person in charge—a woman—said, "Okay, it's late. If you can't call everyone on your team tonight, have your wives do it tomorrow."

I raised my hand.

"Yes, Jen," she said.

"Can I have a wife?" I asked.

The men chuckled, and yet, I'll bet that the next day, their wives did the calls for them. Wait a minute. Who signed up to coach, ladies? Not you. Don't do it! My husband didn't, and I certainly didn't expect him to. I was the coach, not him.

Say, "I Know Nothing!"

Remember Sergeant Schultz? The German soldier in the TV show *Hogan's Heroes* who pretended not to know what Hogan and the other American POWs were up to, saying, "I know nothing"? Be like Sergeant Schultz. Know nothing.

This means that you should not, at any given time, know where the blanket from the couch is, what happened to the Phillips-head screwdriver, or what time the Bears game starts. Because once you become the family's very own human Google, you will have to keep a whole lot of information in your head that there's really no room for, what with all the times of dentist appointments, locations of oatmeal boxes and soccer socks, etc. in there.

I'm not saying you should become completely useless. Somebody's got to remember the pediatrician's phone number and what time the school bus comes. I'm just saying that you need to do your own information triage or else you might as well set up a booth in your kitchen under a sign that reads "Information." And I don't know about you, but I don't want to keep track of my husband's running shoes when I can barely find my own before we rush out in the morning.

Pick Out the Marshmallows

When I was a kid, I spent quite a few afternoons watching reruns of *The Little Rascals* while eating Lucky Charms. (It was the seventies. We didn't know about high-sugar snacks or TV-watching guidelines.) I'd pour handfuls of the cereal into one hand, pick out the marshmallows, and line them up on the arm of the couch. Then I'd make a big ball out of the marshmallows, and eat it.

Think of the chores in your house like Lucky Charms. There's a whole lot of them, but only some of them are truly important. Don't waste your time nagging your husband about the frosted oats kind of chores. You need to concentrate your efforts (and gentle nudging, not nagging) on the colorful marshmallow chores.

Mowing the lawn might be the green clovers of your house. Putting his dirty clothes away could be your pink hearts, while emptying the dishwasher is your yellow moon. Cooking dinner for a houseful of guests? That's your purple horseshoe. And getting up with the kids in the middle of the night, well, that's your pot of gold.

Ask Hubby to do only those things that you consider your marshmallows and you'll find yourself nagging less and doing less around the house.

As for my husband's coat, well, I gave up on that orange star and did one better—I had the closet near the kitchen door enlarged when we remodeled the house. Now he's got the room to fit his big ol' Eddie Bauer coat in there. And I've got one less marshmallow to worry about.

Will You Get to Go Out with Hubby on Saturday Night?

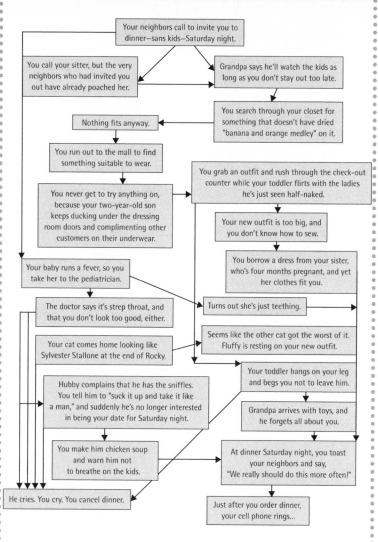

Originally appeared in *Parenting* magazine.

Desperate Housewives Wasn't Written for Preschoolers

It took just one comment from a second grader to make me feel like an idiot. I was wearing my "I coach" sweatshirt, the one with the stick figure who's holding a soccer ball in its, uh, is that technically a hand? And it held a whistle in the other whatever that is.

One of my son's classmates said, "Oh, I have a video game that looks like that," as he pointed to my stick figure. "He shoots."

"Oh!" I replied in that silly sing-song voice that parents use to talk to innocent little children. "He shoots goals, just like you, right?" I asked. "You're a good soccer player."

He looked at me like I was the Village Idiot let out for pottery class before I had to return to the group home. "No," he smirked. "He shoots." Then he held up his fingers like a gun, and shot me with them. And he got me right in the whistle. So I made a mental note: Don't let my son play at his house. After all, his stick figures pack heat.

I had to see for myself what this eight-year-old was talking about, so I Googled "stick figures shoot." Oh, how I wish I hadn't. While online, I discovered a disturbing virtual world where stick figures are programmed to commit all sorts of Soprano-style crimes, including the *Stick Figure Suicides* and the *Killing Spree Series*. Great for Quentin Tarantino's kids, but not for mine.

After I had the misfortune of seeing a stick figure revving up his bloody chainsaw, I decided I needed to visit PBSKids.org, where a few minutes of hanging out with the *CyberChase* kids as they calculated the area of a skateboarding rink made me feel as though I was taking a long, hot, sudsy shower after being dunked into a vat of maggots.

I'd like to think that this eight-year-old's mother wasn't knowingly letting him play *Die in Style,* though I wondered which would have been worse: Letting him play it, or not bothering to see what he's playing at all. Either way I'm not wearing my "I coach" sweatshirt around that kid again. It makes me feel vulnerable, like a victim in *Stabbing in Stickville.*

Cartoons Aren't Just for Kids Anymore

Here's a rule that some in our generation, who grew up watching Bugs Bunny outsmart everyone around him, seem not to understand: Just because a show is animated, doesn't mean it's made for children. Rule of thumb for those of us who grew up when MTV actually played music videos and the most-watched animated shows included *Fat Albert* and *Scooby-Doo*: If it's on Comedy Central, Spike, or Fox, especially after nine p.m., it's not for Junior.

You'd think we'd have figured that out nearly two decades ago when *The Simpsons* first went on the air. When I watched the cartoon in college, I realized this show wasn't Looney Toons. And it still isn't. In the 2005 season premiere of *The Simpsons,* Homer allowed the mafia to film a pornographic movie in his family's home. Hardly the Disney Sunday Movie of our childhood, and yet it aired at eight p.m.—and on a Sunday, no less. And yet, in 2007, the show was ranked third among prime-time shows in the two- through seventeen-year-old demographic. D'oh!

Of course, it's hard to know how many of the kids watching this Rated TV-14 show were under fourteen, but judging by the number of eleven-year-olds who have reviewed *The Simpsons* on CommonSenseMedia.org, I'd guess there are quite a few Bart fans in our middle schools. One math-challenged thirteen-year-old claimed he'd watched the show "since I was seven (four years)." He labeled it the "best TV show ever," and then, after "okay for kids my age?" entered "NO."

"No" is right. And "No Stinkin' Way" should be the ranking for kids under fifteen who watch *South Park,* rated TV-MA for "mature," or perhaps at least "out of braces and algebra class." But they do. One thirteen-year-old reviewer wrote, "This show is pretty bad. My friends and I watch it, though not appropriate for my age." Huh? Mom? Dad? Where are you?

Another eleven-year-old viewer explained how he and his peers manage to watch this show, despite parental controls: "If our parents don't want us to watch it, we are clever enough to hook it off the net and put it in an encrypted folder somewhere deep. We love *South Park* and we don't care." Maybe he plays *Stick Figure Suicides,* too, since he knows how to "hook it off the net" right under his parents' noses.

Not Ready for Prime Time

What was last year's top-rated prime time show among two- to twelve-year-olds? *The Gilmore Girls? The Suite Life of Zach and Cody?* Nope: *Desperate Housewives.* Now more than ever, it's important to screen what your kids watch, or else they'll learn about romance from Wisteria Lane, home to conniving, scantily clad mothers who sleep around and around again.

For every mother who has banned *Arthur* from her kid's TV schedules because he occasionally says "stupid" to refer to home-work, there are ten more who have swung the pendulum so far in the other direction they let their seven-year-olds see PG-13 movies punctuated with words that you wouldn't want to say in front of your grandmother. Parents are *letting* them watch *South Park* and *The Simpsons* and even *Grey's Anatomy*. Sometimes it's just easier to give in and not change the channel.

Teachers, too, have been involved in making sure our kids see what they're not quite ready to see. Some of the R-rated movies that news reports say have been shown in middle and high school classes include *The Departed*, which some professional movie reviewers ranked second only to *Goodfellas* in what the MPAA warned is "strong brutal violence"; the epic *300*, which film critics described using words like "blood lust," "body count," "near naked men," and "a smoking hot sex scene"; and *Brokeback Mountain*, the story of homosexual love that upset one teen's family so much, they sued their school district.

It makes me wonder what happened to the days of film strips about deep-sea creatures. And here, we kids of the seventies and eighties thought an afternoon watching puffer fish expand their faces was a real treat at school. The closest thing we got to "near naked men" was Jacques Cousteau pulling off his scuba suit.

If we can't even trust teachers to filter out the filthy, inappropriate, and just plain wrong for our kids, who can we trust? Not the kids on our school buses, who can—and have—shown R-rated movies and worse on their technological gadgets. Not even their parents, who offer to take our eight-year-olds to PG-13-rated (for fantasy violence, intense battle scenes, and some frightening images) movies for their kid's birthday. ("But Mom. Everybody else is going.")

But consider this: Who's going to stay up with your child tonight when he's got nightmares from the fantasy violence, intense battle scenes, and frightening images?

10 Signs Your Kids Are Watching Too Much Grown-Up TV

1. When they hear The Who sing "Who Are You?" on the radio, it reminds them that the *CSI* season finale is on Thursday night.
2. Your eight-year-old can't figure out what to write in her book report, but she can quote Homer Simpson effortlessly.
3. Your son swears he saw his new fourth-grade teacher in a commercial for *Girls Gone Wild.*
4. Your three-year-old wanders around the house singing the 1-800-MATTRESS jingle played in every commercial break during your favorite soap.
5. When you accuse your second grader of stealing your Häagen-Dazs coffee ice cream, she asks to see latent prints, knowing full well you can't get prints off the icy carton. They said so on *Murder: Real People Solving Real Crimes.*
6. You find out what's happening on *Grey's Anatomy* every time you drive the Girl Scouts carpool.
7. When you forget the code for the child block on your TV, you just ask your first grader, who has memorized it.
8. Everything your eleven-year-old daughter has learned about being a stand-up comic came from watching *Kathy Griffin: Life on the D-List* reruns after school. Also, everything she knows about sex toys and hosting the Gay Porn Awards.
9. Your five-year-old, unlike his grandmother, knows what a "smackdown" is.
10. Your preschooler has been sent home—again—for arresting her classmates for possession while singing, "Bad boys, bad boys, whatcha gonna do?"

Touch That Dial!

Sometimes it's hard to shield your kids from what's on TV. One summer morning, I was in the waiting room at a blood testing center where the TV was tuned to the news. Several children, all under age twelve, were watching the TV with me when the station reported a bombing overseas, blood, gore, and all. Their mother looked up at the TV and sighed. Then she went back to reading *People* magazine ("Paris's Time Behind Bars") while her kids watched a car bomber who was on fire being hosed down by firefighters.

I was frightened by the report, so I can only imagine the feelings of her nine-year-old, who looked like he'd just stumbled into a midnight showing of *Saw*. But what can a mother do when there's a public TV showing not-ready-for-prime-time programming?

Change the channel.

I do it frequently, even when the kids aren't around, because I really don't want to watch *The Jerry Springer Show* when I'm waiting to be stuck with needles. That's painful enough without first watching transvestites argue with housewives. And I certainly don't want the kids to see it. Ever.

Even when there's a sign that says, "Please do not touch the TV controls," I touch the TV controls. At the very least, this mom could have asked the nurse to turn it off. Or she could have moved her brood out of the waiting area until it was their turn. But she, like many mothers faced with public TVs blaring not-exactly-PG shows, seem to think that parental controls work only at home.

You Are the New *TV Guide*

It gets harder every new TV season to find suitable shows for kids. Once the kids outgrow *Dora the Explorer*, there seems to be an absence of decent shows for not-ready-for-MTV kids to watch. A handful of Y-7 shows have entertained my kids, but my older son doesn't want to watch PBSKids anymore, and he just isn't into the Disney Channel.

So, what do we watch with him? HGTV. There's nothing but G and PG shows on that channel, not to mention easy-on-the-eyes commercials about paint and decking. He may not learn the Spanish word for "pineapple," but he could end up a well-paid contractor or a professional organizer.

It makes me long for the days when a kid could just turn on the TV and watch *Batman* reruns until Mom announced dinner. Now, I've got to monitor what they watch by keeping up on the parental control ratings and the real-world mom reviews, all while chopping up the onions and fielding phone calls about soccer practice and breaking up fights about who's sitting where on the couch.

And I fear the future, when my boys will be old enough to watch those shows where people eat live bugs, "hook up" with each other while living in houses with cameras built in every room, and play tennis naked. (I discovered nude sports on Spike one night when I was hoping to tune into *CSI.* Their privates were blacked out, but you could still tell that the men were swinging more than their rackets.)

This is exactly why I think it's dangerous to leave the TV on as background noise and to let kids have televisions in their rooms. It's hard enough to shield them from the gory news stories and obnoxious Cartoon Network shows when you're sitting there watching the TV with them, but once you put it out of sight, you might as well invite the boys from *South Park* over to play with the kids while you mix your evening margaritas. Crap goes in. Crap comes out. And we're the gatekeepers of the crap. Lucky us.

Yet, an Hour in Front of the TV Won't Melt Their Brains

Don't get me wrong: I don't think TV is evil. There are lots of great shows the kids can watch, and they aren't all run by Major League Baseball or PBS. Still, there are some folks who demonize television, or make recommendations that the average mom just can't follow.

The American Academy of Pediatrics (AAP) is among them. The medical organization advises parents to never put a child under age two in front of the TV. But the AAP isn't available to babysit while you make dinner in peace. As far as I'm concerned, that's what Elmo is for.

When my kids were little, after twelve hours of engaging in brain-building activities and mopping up potty training accidents, I know I needed to make my thirty-minute meals without cranky toddlers hanging on my belt loops during the Witching Hour. And since my husband was at work until six, I found a babysitter in the family room who could entertain my children while I threw chicken nuggets in the microwave and attempted to make something for us grown-ups that you wouldn't find on a children's menu at Macaroni Grill. That's right, the TV.

I simply can't sign up for the anti-TV club, the mothers who never let their kids see anything on TV, even something as benign as *Blues Clues*. I find that when kids don't spend much time watching TV, they can be hypnotized by it when they do. While one of my sons, the one who watches *CyberChase* and my collection of *Little Rascals* videos (with parental commentary), isn't drawn to the tube like a moth to a porch light, his brother sometimes is. He doesn't watch much more than *Flip That House* and some Yankees games. So when he stops to stare at *The Deadliest Catch*, having completely forgotten that he came downstairs for a pencil and to show us his latest artwork at night, I have to remind him that he is in the family room with me and not on a king crab boat in the Bering Sea.

This is also what can happen to kids who aren't allowed to watch TV, only worse. They become fixated on what's taboo in their homes, and then they forget all about my kid, whom they're supposed to be playing basketball with outside. Instead, they stand in my family room, staring at the Weather Channel as though they're watching the moon landing for the first time, rather than the jet stream for the Plains, which is nowhere near our New Jersey home anyhow.

TV is not the Evil Empire, but it's not the family-friendly destination it once was, either. Plan your visits accordingly.

Jen's Tips for Protecting the Kids from Naked Tennis on TV, Among Other Things
Screen Out the Mean, the Rude, and the Just Plain Inappropriate

When our kids were sleepless babies and toddlers, my husband and I lost a few years of nighttime channel surfing to colic and diaper management. Every week, we taped three prime-time TV shows to watch whenever we could stay awake long enough to make it to the end of the program, including: *Law & Order, ER,* and the since-canceled *Homicide: Life on the Street.*

When we finally got back to channel surfing after eight p.m., we were shocked to discover people eating worms and other bizarre behavior on the new batch of reality shows, starring the dysfunctional, the rude, the selfish, and the tattooed and half-naked. We cringed and wondered, *What the heck happened to* Mad About You?

When my kids became old enough to handle a remote (without shoving it in their mouths), I programmed my TV's parental controls to block out anything rated higher than TV-G, later upping the limit to TV-Y-7 and then PG. I started reading online reviews from parents and TV watchdog websites, which outline each show's propensity toward violence, sex, language, and what's just plain not appropriate for kids, especially the dysfunctional, the rude, the selfish, and the tattooed and half-naked.

I sometimes cross-reference them between the die-hard religious sites and unsupervised tweens' reviews to get a happy medium type of reality check that usually agrees with my stomach. Finally, I watch some shows myself to decide whether I want my kids to see it or skip it.

Now that my kids are older, I'm losing my viewing thumbprint on them. I'm at the mercy of other parents, who may not have set their internal gauges the same way I have—or at all. So, I have given my kids their own gauges. I've taught my kids not to watch certain shows or to play Rated-T (for Teen) video games at their friends' houses. So far, they've told their playdates what they can't see, as far as I know. And they've even reported it to me when a friend put on a Rated-T Darth Vader game. I told the friend's mom my sons can't play it, and since then, I'm confident that they haven't.

I also discuss movies with other moms to gauge their personal ratings barometer. When one mother told me she couldn't understand why *War of the Worlds* gave her eight-year-old nightmares, I thought of the movie's horrifying scene of bodies floating down the river and decided not to let my kids watch anything at her house.

I might not be able to catch everything, but my kids understand that I'm protecting them from things they're not mature enough yet to see.

Be a Rebel Mom

It's hard to be the only mom who says, "Hey, wait a minute. Maybe my nine-year-old shouldn't be watching *The Simpsons*." Because as soon as you point out to the other mothers on the sidelines at Little League baseball that your daughter never said "crap" until she heard Bart Simpson say it to his father, they're going to move a little farther away from you on the bleachers. It's much easier to be the cool mom who blends in with the others, figuring the kids are fast becoming old enough to handle the pop culture drivel anyhow.

It's also way more work being the watchdog mom who thinks, "Hmmmm. When my kids watch *Rugrats,* they treat me like I'm Naomi Campbell's housekeeper and I need good cell phone whipping. Maybe they shouldn't watch that." Because then you have to not only take away their access to *Rugrats,* but also spend gobs of time and effort channeling their energy into something less obnoxious, and therefore less appealing to your offspring. That can take persistence when you've already got way too much on your plate as usual, plus it requires the ability to repeatedly say the word "no" despite how much your kids wear you down like terrorists trying to get a little uranium for their "power plants." (They've mastered sleep deprivation, haven't they, and the UN has declared that a form of torture.)

When you've had the kind of patience-sucking day that leaves you wishing you could make yourself a gin and tonic, lie on the couch, and watch *Celebrity Poker* until you doze off and drool on your new throw pillows, it's hard to be the Rebel Mom. It's far easier to park the kiddies in front of the TV—whatever the heck you can find on TV because frankly, you don't care—and go reheat last night's leftover pizza, praying no one talks to you until at least the next commercial break.

But if you take that extra step of blocking out the bad stuff on TV now, you make it easier the next time you have one of those days to get the kids to watch something that doesn't teach them to treat grown-ups like useless minions in their daily dramas and, perhaps, go play Uno. It's just a matter of making rules for yourself and sticking with them, no matter how much you want to hide with an umbrella drink in the basement where you keep your scrapbook supplies or behind the sale rack at Kohl's.

Don't Treat the TV Like the Anti-Christ Has Set Up Shop in Your Family Room

Madonna reportedly doesn't allow her kids to watch TV. In interviews, she has spit out this fact as though she is protecting her children from viewing the filthy living habits of the heathens who live outside her sprawling home's gates when, really, she probably doesn't want little Lourdes to see her in an old concert, dressed in a pointy-breasted bustier, "dancing" with men wearing not much more than a swath of Spandex and matching suspenders.

While I am disappointed that so much of decent television went down the toilet at the end of the twentieth century, I do not agree with her. I don't think TV is the sole cause of society's current downward spiral toward moral depravity. Rather, there are lots of very well written, clever, and formidable shows on TV. I just don't think my kids should see them all. Not yet, anyhow.

It pains me to hear that kids as young as eight have watched one of my favorite shows, *CSI*—a show that makes me close my eyes to get through half of the autopsy scenes. But I don't think the show should be taken off the air and replaced with reruns of *Little House on the Prairie,* either.

I believe that once you start training your kids to believe that the TV is the Devil's publicist, they will want to tune in more, not less. I mean, remember what happened to those kids in *Footloose* after the mean minister banned dancing in their little Midwestern town? Turns out, everybody gotta cut loose. Footloose. And everybody gotta see *American Idol* now and then, or at least Wimbledon. And a half-hour of *Dora the Explorer* isn't going to hurt your kids' brains. *Es bueno, si?*

In the winter months, my son likes to wind down from school with a little Mom-approved TV at 5 p.m. He can watch another episode at 5:30, or he can go play with his brother. I don't hover over the final moments of the show, reminding him that his thirty to sixty minutes of TV for the day are about to end, thereby implying that if he gets a minute more, his mind will start oozing out of his ears. Rather, I taught him to turn off the TV when he's done with it. That way, he feels like he's in charge, and I don't have to get the PBSKids jingle stuck in my head.

I've noticed that he's less interested in television when the weather is nice outside, and that he can watch it for hours when he's at home with strep throat. I used to feel pressure to turn their sick days into yet another educational opportunity, or at least a board game extravaganza. But I know I feel better when I watch a few hours of *Dirty Jobs* peppered with some *Ellen* when I'm sick, so what's wrong with a couple days a year of *SpongeBob SquarePants* marathons? After all, none of us has turned to a life of crime because of it. So far, anyway.

TV and Your Family: What Kind of Mom Are You?

1. *When the kids are bored, I . . .*
   a. sit at the kitchen table and teach them how to make lampshades with cut-outs of kittens or smiling dump trucks, even if I've got a ton of other things to do.
   b. let them watch a half-hour or so of whatever's on PBS or Nick Jr.
   c. point to the TV and tell them to leave me alone.

2. *When I've got to make dinner and the kids are off the wall, I . . .*
   a. turn it into a teachable moment, where even the youngest kids help me get dinner on the table, even if it means breaking up fights over who gets to put the Winnie the Pooh plate out for the baby.

b. secretly wish that the folks at the American Academy of Pediatrics, who declared that children under two shouldn't watch TV, would stop by to entertain my kids while I finish making the lasagna.

c. thank God for TiVo.

3. *When the kids walk in during the most riveting part of my favorite TV-14 show, I . . .*

a. turn off the TV and go play a board game with them.

b. quickly flip over to the Food Network and remind them that my favorite show is on TV, so they need to leave.

c. tell them to be quiet while I find out if *The Closer's* Kyra Sedgwick can get a confession out of this week's child murderer.

4. *I think those portable DVD players for your car are . . .*

a. taking away from my children's view of nature and, uh, strip mall parking lots.

b. fine for long trips, but do my kids really need to watch fourteen minutes of *Shrek the Third* en route to Costco?

c. better than a soundproofed partition behind the driver's seat.

5. *What do you think about TVs in the kids' bedrooms?*

a. Never! We don't even own a TV.

b. Only when they're old enough to watch HBO, which is well after puberty hits.

c. If it means I never have to hear Hannah Montana sing again, then I'm all for them.

6. *What do you do when a questionable commercial comes on during the ball game?*

    a. We never watch sports on TV, but my kids can check the scores in the *New York Times*.

    b. I flip the channel over to HGTV and watch people pick out paint colors until the game's back on.

    c. Huh? We wait for the game to come back on. Whadaya mean?

7. *If you walk into our house at any time, you'll find the TV...*

    a. in the attic, unplugged and dusty. I keep telling my husband to give it away, though I'm really not sure it's an appropriate gift for a nonprofit organization that caters to children or the infirm.

    b. off, unless there's something in particular one of us wants to watch.

    c. on, even if only the dog is watching the news.

8. *If you answered:*

    Mostly A's—you have something in common with Madonna.

    Mostly B's—you've missed parts of your favorite shows, but your kids haven't.

    Mostly C's—you've no doubt seen the commercials for parental controls by now, and yet haven't found the buttons on your remote.

Watch Access Hollywood for Britney Spears Updates, Not Parenting Tips

The year I became a mother, there was a celebrity baby boom. Everyone, from Heather Locklear to Harry Connick Jr., from Julio Iglesias to Jennie Garth, and from Spike Lee to Faith Hill, became parents or added to their families in 1997. And they made it look so good—and so easy.

That year, *FHM* readers voted Teri Hatcher the "Sexiest Woman in the World"—and yet, she was pregnant most of that year. I'd have been lucky to be selected as the "Best-Looking Woman on Bed Rest in a Three-Block Radius for the Month of March, 1997." And that would have been a stretch.

Bed rest isn't exactly a beauty routine, but I did learn a lot that month watching celebrities hawking skin care products on QVC. The number one lesson I learned is that it's great to have a makeup expert on staff. Also, that soft-focus camera lens has been so kind to stars like Paula Zahn, Cybill Shepherd, and even Lou Dobbs. Where can I get one?

In the years that followed, Hollywood made motherhood look glamorous and exciting. Julia Roberts, expecting twins, appeared on *Oprah* to let everyone know, "I haven't thrown up at all!" Expecting her first baby, *Access Hollywood* reporter Nancy O'Dell appeared in paparazzi photos wearing short dresses and sexy high boots, radiant with mommy anticipation and a liberal application of bronzer. The celebrity magazines featured these and other famous moms-to-be showing off their "baby bumps" to a generation of new moms more likely to be lugging around "baby buttes." *Us Weekly* practically screamed about Tori Spelling's "Baby Love" from its clearly retouched cover photo of the actress and her newborn. (Nobody who undergoes the major surgery that is a C-Section ends up with skin as smooth and even as a four-year-old's and eyes as clear as the wax figures' at Madame Tussaud's unless there's a full frontal makeover or some heavy-duty retouching.)

To mere mortals like us, celebrities make mommyhood look oh-so-fabulous. We wonder why we can't look that good while grabbing our big ol' bellies—on national TV, even!—and setting our faces into that permanent smile that makes celebrity mommies look impossibly happy and yet a little bit stoned. Why?

Because we don't have a staff, that's why. Hollywood's smoke and mirrors hide the fact that hired help will probably get up with the baby at night. You'll never look as good as *Desperate Housewives* star Marcia Cross after she gave birth to twins at forty-four, because, chances are, she had a nanny, a stylist, a makeup artist, a dietician, a personal trainer, and a full night's sleep or a dozen. You have, what? A dusty yoga DVD and a pantry full of mac n' cheese.

And don't forget that these photos are all staged. All you have to do is check out the celebrity gossip blogs, which revel in displaying rather unattractive photos of celebrities, like the one of a very pregnant Britney Spears in that side-view shot no mother-to-be should ever be subjected to. See? It's not all that glamorous after all. So why are you so riveted?

Hollywood: It Ain't Kansas

Unlike most celebrities, it's likely that you have a firm grasp on down-to-earth issues, such as whether Target has the diapers you're looking for or if your toddler might have a meltdown before you make it through the checkout line. Celebrities, though, have an entirely different life, one where they give out $600 pearl necklaces as party favors at their baby showers, like Tori Spelling did.

Spelling also thought it would be oh-so-cute to feature childhood favorites on the menu at her coed baby shower, such as grilled cheese sandwiches, tuna melts, mini corn dogs, and pigs in a blanket. The menu, presented on an Etch-a-Sketch (how kitschy!), offered up a dessert that included blueberry Popsicles, just like in my backyard in August.

Any normal mother would know that this would become her diet for the next thirteen years, and would therefore stick to foods that you can't order at Chuck E. Cheese while she still can. But Spelling and her giggly gaggle of celebrity friends will continue to lunch on arugula and goat cheese salads at Spago in Beverly Hills long after the baby shower ends (and Spelling's people packed up the Bugaboos in the Escalade and drove them home so they could get started on the thank-you notes).

To celebs, pigs in a blanket are just so darn cute! To the rest of us, it's what we buy in bulk at Costco. And your baby shower isn't so much your opportunity to show off your hostessing skills and whimsical decorating abilities as it is your last chance to sit down and eat cake with both hands.

You can't compare your home life to celebrity lifestyles, either. When Britney Spears needs a break from motherhood, she goes out clubbing all night with her pals Paris and Lindsay, and, apparently, no underpants. When you need a break from being a mom, you beg your mother to take the baby for a few hours so you can go out for burgers and Mojitos at Houlihan's with your husband.

When you get home (at 9:15 p.m.), you go straight to bed because you know you've got maybe eighty-five minutes until the baby wakes you up. Also, because your post-partum alcohol limit is a half a drink, and you drank the whole thing, didn't you? Won't you be sorry tomorrow.

America's Royalty, Not Exactly Pillars of Society

You devoured the photos of elaborate celebrity wedding extravaganzas, and now, you're on baby bump watch along with the editors at *US Weekly* and the girls who work the checkout line at Safeway. Oh, the glamorous lives of celebrities. If only you, too, could live like they do. Are you sure you really want to?

Two words for you: Alec Baldwin.

Sure, we know about celebrity familial woes because they're broadcast on *Entertainment Tonight* and spammed across YouTube, but think about it: There seems to be a very high percentage of celebrities who do dumb things like call their eleven-year-old kid a "thoughtless pig" on voice mail.

Normally, you see that sort of thing only on *Cops* and maybe at that house down the street that has rottweilers chained up outside. (Really, how many of your neighbors drive around with a baby in their lap?)

And the spouses of stars aren't much better. Anne Heche said in court papers that her estranged husband, Coley Laffoon (which I assume rhymes with "buffoon"), claimed to be a stay-at-home father, but actually left their five-year-old son, Homer, at home "with nannies and babysitters while he play(ed) ping-pong, backgammon, and poker and view(ed) pornography online." Perhaps you can see why you shouldn't get your parenting tips from *Access Hollywood* or the "Baby Lust" spread in *People* magazine.

Certainly, there are wonderful celebrity parents, such as Will Smith and Jada Pinkett, and Demi Moore and Bruce Willis (and

Ashton Kutcher, too—everybody move in for a group photo) appear to be. But the celebrity parents you mostly hear about are the ones making headlines on TMZ.com in articles about court papers, "blow-ups," and nasty voice mails to their tweenage children.

Real-World Pregnancy	Celebrity Pregnancy
You call your parents and then your hubby's to announce you're pregnant.	You call your publicist and then your agent to announce you're pregnant on *Showbiz Tonight* and maybe *Letterman.*
You send your sister up to her attic to retrieve her maternity clothes for you.	You send your assistant to that cute shop on Rodeo Drive to retrieve maternity clothes for you.
You subscribe to *American Baby.*	You set up a photo shoot with *American Baby.*
You call your OB/GYN to find out how soon you can have your gender-determining ultrasound so you can start painting the nursery.	You call your OB/GYN to find out how soon you can induce so you can start getting back in shape.
Your best friend throws you a surprise baby shower at Macaroni Grill. You receive a Graco stroller, a Baby Bjorn to carry the baby in, and enough baby clothes to get you through the first three months.	Kate Hudson throws you a surprise baby shower at her house in Malibu. You receive three Peg Perego strollers (one for each house), a Baby Bjorn for the nanny to carry the baby in, and enough baby clothes to fill three closets.

You pack your makeup on the day your water breaks so you can look your best for your family's photos.	You pack up your makeup artist on the day you induce so you can look your best for the paparazzi's photos.
After nearly a month, you finally send out baby announcements.	After nearly a month, your assistant finally finishes sending out baby announcements.
You make your first public appearance at your baby's one-month checkup. You wear your old college sweatshirt and your husband's jeans, because—rats!—that's all you can fit into.	You make your first public appearance on the red carpet at your movie premiere. You wear Oscar de la Renta in a size four, because—rats!—that's all you can fit into.

It's Just Mad!

And then there are the celebrity moms who raise the parenting bar impossibly high, higher than even the creator of *Baby Einstein* and the person who decided that newborns should be attended to on-demand and not on schedule.

Sarah Jessica Parker is one of those celebrities, even though she complained about it, lamenting, "I hate the fact that pregnant women are now expected to get straight back into shape after having their babies. It's just mad."

Yes, how mad it was when she slinked back into her size-zero clothes for *Sex and the City* after giving birth in 2002. Or two years later, when she flounced around TV ads for Gap, singing, "I enjoy being a girl!"

After you watch that commercial a few dozen times during *Oprah,* you may think that if you buy that frilly pink shirt that

Carrie Bradshaw wore in the Gap ad, you'll enjoy being a girl, too. Until your frilly pink shirt winds up with spit-up and what appears to be strained peas encrusted into the buttons. Then you realize that someone else must be carrying around her kids for her.

Catherine Zeta-Jones reportedly agreed with Parker's sentiment. "I think it's awful, this competition between actresses who just had a baby to see who's first to get back to their normal weight. I find this wave of super-skinny women scary."

The magazines applaud Zeta-Jones for her curves, which make her, what? A size six? And yet she's our normal mom model from Hollywood. Now that's scary. She also reportedly was caught on camera smoking while pregnant. Maybe that's how she kept those curves so manageable.

While the celebs are flouncing around Beverly Hills, you're eating the SpongeBob-shaped mac n' cheese your kid didn't finish and reading about Victoria Beckham's (aka Posh Spice) amazing size-four figure after having three kids. When she was spotted reading *Skinny Bitch*, a diet book that declares, "Soda is liquid Satan," that book's sales shot up tremendously. Posh is influential. Posh is posh. Posh is a skinny bitch. And you want to be one, too.

But Posh has also admitted to suffering from "a few food issues." For a while, she lived on vegetables and nothing else. While your vegetables-only diet might be McDonald's fries, she can't get away with that. Not with hordes of paparazzi following her every move, even as police pulled her over outside (where else?) a Hollywood shopping area. It's no wonder celebrity moms have gone mad for dropping their pregnancy pounds. Everybody's watching them.

What if paparazzi watched you from the bushes as you returned home from the maternity ward after thirty hours of labor? What if VH1 nominated you for their "Celebrity Fat Club?" What if an entire nation branded you "fat" after your performance in front of millions on the MTV Video Music Awards? Maybe celebrity isn't what you truly would like, after all. The money, yes. But not the fishbowl life. It's just plain mad.

Jen's Tips for Getting Over Celebrity Mom Envy
Remember, Madonna Is Not a Role Model

Would you invite someone who simulates sex in front of thousands to your Mommy and Me class? "Hi everyone. This is my new friend. On weekends, she wears a bustier and sings about being 'touched for the very first time' in front of screaming teenagers. Oh! And she's written a children's book!"

Of course not, so don't let Madonna into your home, either. If you've ever been on "baby bump" watch, wondering whether Katie Holmes would pop out more offspring for her couch-jumping husband, you're thinking way too much about people whose lives are nothing like yours.

And chances are, your tween is, too. When Anna Nicole Smith's drug overdose took over the headlines—in a time of war, no less—it was difficult to avoid the relentless "news." But you don't need to aid and abet celebrity-mom rubbernecking by bringing home, say, *US Weekly*'s investigative report, "The Dramatic Last Year of Anna Nicole Smith's Life." Your tween already knows way too much about Anna Nicole Smith, and so do you. Don't keep it on the coffee table.

If celebrity watching is your favorite spectator sport, that's fine. Just rein it in and keep it in perspective for you and for your children. Wouldn't you rather be your kid's role model than let her look up to the likes of Britney Spears? You're more qualified as a role model than many celebrities, because, chances are, you've never dangled your baby over the side of a balcony or tooled down the highway with your baby in your lap. Plus, you wear underwear in public, not to mention on camera. Take the focus off people who don't make good role models and put it where it belongs—on you and your family.

Don't Enter the Competition

Trying to compete with celebrity mothers who are wearing size-two dresses on the red carpet just nine weeks after giving birth is like entering the National Spelling Bee after studying nothing more than a word-a-day calendar and the ingredients list on a box of fruit roll ups (Acetylated Diglycerides, A-C-E-T-Y-L-A-T-E-D D-I-G-L-Y-C-E-R-I-D-E-S, Acetylated Diglycerides).

You're out of your league, Mom.

No matter how much *E! True Hollywood Story* portrays celebrity moms as "hands-on" and "dedicated," all the images of these famous glam-moms pushing strollers down Rodeo Drive don't come close to what your average day is like. When they're done pushing the stroller, a maid puts it away while a nanny puts the child away and the celeb-mom goes for a much-needed soak in the tub where no one talks to her through the bathroom door.

Yet when you return from pushing the stroller, you change diapers, dig up snacks, answer the phone, schedule an appointment for the septic guy to drop by to figure out what that awful smell is in the backyard, unearth the Cub Scouts schedule for your husband, break up a fight over Tickle Me Elmo, clean up the dog's living room accident (which is really his continual comment on how much he despises sharing your attention with the kids), and attempt to take a quick pee, even though kids are talking to you through the bathroom door. And it ain't glamorous.

You don't have time to get yourself into a size-two dress (as if you were ever in one in the first place), and you're not going to be invited to walk down a red carpet anytime soon anyhow. You're only going to drive yourself crazy if you try to compete with the stars when the playing field is far from level.

Quit Staring

A few years ago, I was photographed for a fashion magazine— yes, a fashion magazine—for an article called something like "What Your Hair Says about You." I didn't know my hair could talk, but it turns out that my 'do says I'm a "sassy mom" without a lot of time to do my hair. Why I needed a fashion magazine to tell me this, I don't know. But I sort of fell into the shoot by accident, and I thought it would be fun.

But when I arrived at the photo shoot, both the makeup artist and the hair stylist seemed very, very concerned about a scar I have next to my eye. Before then, nobody had mentioned it much since I had fallen into the coffee table at age six and had to get fourteen stitches. After the scar healed, it just became part of my look, and I rarely think of it.

But these women acted as though they were going to have to figure out a way to hide a third arm growing from my chest or something. So, they promised to retouch me. I thought they meant that they'd retouch the scar out of the photo later on, but no, they meant they were going to spray-paint my face with an electronic makeup sprayer much like the painters you find at an auto body shop. In short, it was like an episode of *Pimp My Mom.*

By the time the magazine came out, I looked way, way better on paper than I'd ever looked in person, largely because my face had been spackled and my photo altered. I looked at the photo and realized something very odd: I was jealous of me. Not me, really, but the airbrushed, primped, fussed-over me who can't possibly keep that up without the aid of New York fashion experts.

So I don't bother to try. And I'm much happier for it. You will be, too, once you realize that the difference between you and celebrity moms is spray paint and a doting staff of experts— experts who would be very, very concerned about the flaws you hardly even notice.

The Family Life,
According to Hollywood

- Boy meets girl.
- Boy leaves wife for girl, who leaves boyfriend for boy.
- Boy and girl show up at Hollywood movie premiere with brand-new tattoos of each other's names on their arms, confirming rumors of their new love.
- Boy's ex-wife reveals in court papers, and in an exclusive interview with *Extra,* his penchant for transvestite prostitutes and jumbo buckets of KFC wings at midnight.
- Boy and girl announce baby due in five months.
- Girl doesn't look like she's that pregnant at all, and frankly, it's annoying to mere mortal moms who don't have stylists and personal trainers watching over their so-called baby bumps 24/7.
- Boy and girl announce birth of a baby boy, whom they name Radicchio, because it sounds to them like a character in a Shakespeare play and also was served on their first date at Spago.
- Girl appears on cover of *People* magazine with her one-month-old baby, looking like she just stepped out of a Gap ad in size-four khakis and a snug-fitting T-shirt under the headline "Back in My Jeans Already!" It's *People's* highest-selling newsstand cover ever.
- Boy gets arrested for soliciting a transvestite prostitute. Tells *Us Weekly* it was the "stress of new fatherhood" and "foggy glasses" that caused his misjudgment.
- Boy and girl have "secret wedding" for five hundred guests. They sell the rights to their wedding photos to British celebrity rag *OK!* for two million dollars and an exclusive interview with baby Raddichio, as soon as he can talk.

- Rumors circulate on Celebrity Baby Blog that girl is pregnant again. She appears on *Oprah* to officially make the announcement and to plug her new clothing line for toddlers, Bambino Couture. Just $79.99 for the cute overalls with the truck embroidered on the bib!
- Boy and girl announce the birth of their baby girl, whom they name Frisée, to keep with the lettuce theme and also because it sounds like the name of a sexy French girl, like a new Lolita, which they, of course, think is wonderful.
- Girl appears on cover of *People* in a bikini with both kids under the headline, "I've never been happier in my life!"
- Girl divorces boy, citing irreconcilable differences. Also, transvestite prostitutes and dozens of empty KFC buckets strewn about their Malibu home.
- Boy sues for joint custody and loses, after drunken rampage through a Chuck E. Cheese where police had to cuff him in the ball pit.
- Divorce is finalized. Girl finds new boy, a rap star who is best known for simulating sex on stage with a girl he didn't know was only fifteen. (He swears!) Boy finds new girl (he swears!) prostitute.

SECRET TWELVE

Don't Treat Fine Restaurants Like a McDonald's PlayPlace

I was wearing a dress. Finally. And makeup and sexy slingback shoes that would certainly get filled with wood chips on the playground before I could even make it to the monkey bars. Only this time, I wasn't going anywhere with my kids.

My husband and I had made reservations at a nice restaurant, the kind with cloth napkins, food made with chutney (whatever that is), and waiters who know how to open a bottle of champagne without first shaking it up and aiming it at someone else. For one night, we felt like grown-ups.

We sat down at our table, put our napkins on our laps, and opened our mouths to talk about mature subjects like career choices and *Law & Order: SVU*. And then we heard it: "Mommy! I want chicken nuggets!" My head swung around like Linda Blair's in *The Exorcist*. I counted one, two, three kids, including a baby, who were seated at a table near the kitchen.

My husband and I looked at each other as though our box seats at Yankee Stadium had been suddenly relocated to the bleachers next to a big man with a bigger splashing beer who's yelling, "Hey Clemens! My grandmother can throw better than you!"

After months of Saturday evenings spent playing Old Maid with the kids, we'd finally gotten a night out for some much-needed couple time only to discover that other parents thought the four-star restaurant serving crab and shiitake-stuffed snapper was, in fact, a Chuck E. Cheese.

Check, please!

Our generation of parents spends more time with its children than any other generation in the past fifty years, perhaps longer. Super Moms are pros at it, spending rainy Saturdays watching animated movies about talking cars or rats or fish with their children.

But dragging the kiddies to places where they shouldn't go is purely Slacker Mom territory. It's easier on Mom, but not necessarily better for the kids. "No Child Left Behind" doesn't mean that other grown-ups should have to put up with your kids running around the dining room while you enjoy your crème brûlée.

Even in this child-centric era, there's still room for Adults Only, and your kids just aren't invited. Believe me, your neighbors don't think it's cute that your two-year-old is tipping over hors d'oeuvres trays at their black-tie New Year's Eve party while you knock back glasses of Korbel and pretend you don't know her. Just because you put her in a nice dress doesn't mean you should bring her along to a party for grown-ups.

"But what if I can't find a babysitter?" you cry. "What if I don't live near family who can help out?"

Two words: Stay home.

And then there are the squirming toddlers at shows geared toward bigger kids. Even my third grader couldn't understand why anyone would bring a three-year-old to see *Chitty Chitty Bang Bang* on Broadway. After he watched the three-year-old announce that he wanted to go on stage and "get in the car, Mommy!" my son turned to me and asked, "Why would you bring a little kid here?" I replied, "Because there was no more room in their garbage can for a hundred and fifty dollars."

There's a reason Disney recommends its Broadway productions for ages six and up, and it's not to make your life more difficult if you've got one kid under six and another over six. It's because three-year-olds will want to climb into the car while everyone else just wants to watch the show.

When your kids get older and can behave themselves appropriately, go ahead and bring them along to a nice restaurant, if you don't mind paying fifteeen dollars for a hamburger and fries, and take them to see *Mary Poppins* on Broadway. (Especially if Grandma is buying the tickets. Thanks, Mom!) Until then, though, Chuck E. Cheese awaits you.

Remember That Guy Who Sleeps Next to You?

I don't mean the one in feety pajamas who keeps sneaking into your bed in the wee hours of the morning. I mean the man who danced the first dance with you at your wedding, to Celine Dion's "My Heart Will Go On," never once making a snide comment about how your wedding song is the theme from a movie about a sinking ship. I mean Hubby. Remember him?

Perhaps you haven't paid as much attention to him since the baby was born, in part because you've been really busy changing diapers and in part because the love you feel for your child far surpasses anything you've felt for your husband since, oh, ever. After all, you'd die for your kids, but not for your husband, as that would leave your kids motherless. And who would do that?

So you put your marriage on autopilot, figuring that if it doesn't crash into a mountain, all is well. The kids require so much of your energy and supervision that the two of you have become more like bouncers than spouses; you're constantly on guard, ready to detain the unruly and the rowdy.

Or maybe your husband is more like a third child to you. No doubt you're frustrated by having to clean up after someone who's more than three feet tall. And sometimes it's hard to feel intimate with someone who leaves his dirty underwear on the bathroom floor for you to trip over in the morning.

Perhaps he's more of an afterthought, in line after the kids, the house, the dog, the bills, the laundry, the dirty floors, the class trip, the pediatrician's appointment, etc. If your time and energy were like a car's gas tank, your husband would have to wait until someone hikes a few miles down the highway to fill up your spare gas can.

Or maybe your kids' schedules keep you so busy you just don't have time for each other, except to wave while in passing, one off to the pee-wee soccer game, and the other en route to flag football practice. You've become your kids' chauffeurs. Hey, maybe you'll run into each other at the Exxon station.

Here's something to think about when you're taking the kids out in the stroller so your husband can get some work done around the house: Your children will leave you someday, but your husband won't—or will he?

How can he enjoy you for who you are when your conversations with him usually sound more like a flight plan?

"Did you pick up the juice boxes like I asked?" you ask.

"Check," he replies.

"Did you put air in the van's tires and scrape that sticky gunk off the door handle?"

"Check."

"Diaper bag?"

"Check."

"Credit card bill?"

"Check. Roger. Over."

Granted, it's tough to have a thoughtful conversation about, say, whether to refinance the mortgage when you're both busy refilling cups at dinner, trying to find Junior's baseball cleats ten minutes before game time, and chasing half-naked, potty training toddlers down the hall. Frankly, it's a wonder you found time to make more than one kid in the first place.

"Me" Time	"What about Me?" Time
Reading the newspaper	Reading just the weather report and the schedule for animated G- and PG-rated movies
Taking a long leisurely bath with bubbles, candles, and Andrea Bocelli on your built-in CD player	Shaving only up to the hem of your Capri pants (who's gonna see it?) while returning Barbie's head to her body and listening to The Wiggles
Getting a hot stone massage at a spa	Emptying the pebbles from your Keds
Going out for a romantic dinner with your husband	Meeting your husband at the Burger King drive-through, where you switch kids for the next round of activities
Meeting friends for a Girls' Night Out	Meeting friends at the Girl Scouts spaghetti dinner and bake sale. Don't forget to bring the lemon squares and plastic forks!

If Momma Ain't Happy, Ain't Nobody Happy

Face it: You go to the dentist so you have an excuse to put your feet up. When every moment of every day is all about your kids, how could you have time for yourself except to steal it? And should you really have time for yourself?

Yes.

Like a Major League Baseball pitcher, Mom is the most important player on the field, or in this case, in the house. Unlike the pitcher, however, she rarely gets a break between games to rest her arm, or her head, or her tired, tired body. And so, like the Energizer Bunny, she just keeps on going. And going. And going, until the kids move out or she crashes like a remote control airplane that runs out of gas over the swimming pool.

As I mentioned earlier, only celebrities get to cite "exhaustion" as a valid reason for wiping their calendars clear and hiding in their bedrooms with the shades drawn. But they've got someone else to pick up the kids at choir practice and mop the kitchen floor. The average mom, however, does not.

Like the T-shirt says, if Momma ain't happy, ain't nobody happy. Because a relentlessly tired mom is a cranky mom, and a cranky mom is just plain miserable to be around. If you're a stay-at-home mom, you might say, "But this is my job. I need to be with the kids all the time."

Contrary to popular belief, nobody needs to be on the job upwards of one hundred hours a week without time off. Even OSHA has rules about workers' break time. And where's your break time? The nineteen seconds between when you close the car door for your kids and open yours? The minute-and-a-half it takes you to scoot down the driveway and get the mail? The thirty-seven seconds before someone realizes that Mommy is sitting down in the bathroom and must need company?

If you're a working mom, you might say, "But I'm gone from my kids all day. I can't justify being without them any longer." If your time and soul are being split between your boss and your kids, maybe you can justify some me time, and I don't mean the forty-seven minutes you spend sitting in traffic, reading bumper stickers with such bon mots as, "I don't mind coming to work, but that eight-hour wait to go home is a bitch!" I mean real me time, like the kind you used to get before you started your work–home juggling act.

Jen's Tips for Taking the Focus off the Kids and Putting It Back on You
Children: Leave Home Without Them
No, don't park them home alone in front of the TV with a bag of Cheese Doodles and the remote. Find a sitter or a neighbor or a relative who can watch your kids while you go out. You don't have to have big plans or spend a lot of money. Just get out.

When our kids were little, we didn't get much sleep, but we made sure we got out now and then. One Saturday night, my husband, Pete, and I left the kids with our babysitter and neighbor, Nina, and went to a coffee shop, where we ordered super grande lattes and then sat outside on a bench. What did we do with our date night? We spent it watching people park their cars.

"Oh, that Buick went around the block again," I said.

"Look at that parallel parking job," Pete admired.

"Oh! They're fighting over that space," I pointed out.

Okay, it wasn't exactly a big night on the town, but we couldn't very well have gone to the movies or we'd have fallen asleep as soon as the lights went out. And we didn't want to stay home, either. Our little reality show, *Park It!*, was all we could handle. But at least we got out of the house.

Friends of ours have had a standing weekly date night since their first child was born. We probably couldn't pull that off, because we just didn't have that much to talk about when the kids were little (unless it had to do with parking, of course). Besides, I often didn't have the energy come Friday to get dressed up and go out. But we always took up babysitting offers from both sets of grandparents.

We were tired, not crazy.

When we can't get out without the kids, we find a place that welcomes children, somewhere that hands out crayons with children's menus or free Pokémon T-shirts for kids under fourteen. Chili's or Yankee Stadium, for example. Not Tavern on the Green or Lincoln Center.

Learn from the Masters of "Me Time"

A friend of mine once confided in me that she wished her husband would just drop off his paycheck once a week and then go live somewhere else. He couldn't handle the kids and their whining, and she couldn't stand being in the middle. Besides, they didn't have time for each other anymore.

It's easy to feel resentment toward your husband after the kids are born, especially when, for so many women, motherhood adds stress and exhaustion that doesn't seem to affect Daddy as much. But I think we could all learn a lesson from fathers.

One weekday morning, I was finishing up my breakfast when my husband, who was waiting for the neighbor to pick him up and take him to work, entered the kitchen. He had about ten minutes until he would leave, so what did he do? Empty the dishwasher? Re-fold the blankets on the couch? Fill out permission slips? No, he flipped through a magazine like someone waiting for an oil change at an auto body shop.

Naturally, this drove me insane. If I had ten minutes until I had to leave, I'd fill that time with minor chores. But he took that time to peruse *Bon Appetit*. And that's when it hit me: A woman's work is never done, but a man's work is punctuated by moments of downtime. No wonder fathers rarely seem as frazzled as we are. They take breaks.

Chances are, unless you ask him to, your husband is not going to wipe the crumbs off the counter (if he even sees them) or take the time to figure out if the kids' swim goggles from last season still fit. He is hard-wired to focus on one thing at a time, even if that one thing is as useless to your family as how to cook coconut basmati rice.

This is not part of his evil plot to make you blow your top. It's just how he is, and frankly, you should try it sometime. It's so much easier than fretting over whether the kids will be hot in long sleeves today or if you remembered to start the clothes dryer. Let go of a few inconsequential things, and you'll feel a lot better.

Put Some "Me Time" in Your Calendar—in Ink

Every summer, my mom and I disappear to a spa for a few days while my mother-in-law watches the kids, and my husband gets to watch all the Food Network shows he can cram into a few nights while I'm away.

It's become a tradition we all look forward to. My kids love being spoiled by their grandparents, who love spending a few days making forts from boxes and taking the kids ice skating indoors on a ninety-degree day. My mother and I love the time to bond, not to mention the hot stone massages and the fancy dinners. And my husband loves to watch his *Iron Chef* marathons without my pleas to change the channel to something more interesting than a race to reduce sauces.

But I don't wait an entire year to get some "me time." I've built it in to just about every day since I first discovered that being able to say an entire paragraph uninterrupted would become as scarce as curse-free dialogue in *The Sopranos*.

When my boys were very little, I'd put them both down for a nap and then sit down to eat lunch—with both hands!—while watching repeats of *The Daily Show* on TV. (Naturally, I hadn't seen any of them during their original airings at eleven p.m. That was past my bedtime.)

This was my time to feel like a grown-up again, even if I twitched like a nervous horse every time I heard a noise on the baby monitors. I usually zonked out before the end of the show, having been up much of the night with one kid or another. But dammit, after a morning of singing the Barney "Clean-up Song," I was going to laugh at intelligent (and okay, often sophomoric) adult humor about the government, thick books I didn't have the time to read, and the errs of big business. This was *my time,* after all!

When friends told me they spent naptime making beds, folding laundry, making phone calls, and checking email, I thought they were all nuts. Who cares if the socks are all matched up when you've got a chance to take a break from the relentlessness of motherhood? All I know is, nobody remembers whether my sheets were changed as frequently as they could have been. But they do remember how damn tired I was back then. I needed the break.

Make a to-do list that's all about you. I know that's hard to do, because you're probably used to putting your haircuts and OB/GYN check-ups at oh, about 103rd on your list, somewhere after taking the dog to the groomer and buying new dishtowels for the kitchen. Include fun stuff like seeing movies that aren't animated and wandering around the bookstore, alone, without ever setting foot in the children's section.

Then take some of those things—especially the fun stuff— and put them on your real to-do list and your calendar as though they're as important as your kids' pediatrician's appointments and the trip to the zoo. Because unless you want to burn out before the kids leave home for good, they *are* as important.

The Mom's Almanac

We are pleased to offer our guide to making your life easier, providing calculated predictions and forecasts about your children's behavior, from sunny to surly, and warm to wild. From its humble beginnings back in 1808, the *Mom's Almanac* has been outfitting mothers with the kind of information they need to get through their days (and months) with children underfoot.

General Mothering Outlook for the Month Ahead:

1st–3rd: Unsettled, with gusty temper tantrums blowing in just when you thought you were going to make it through that fancy gift shop—the one with the disapproving old ladies staring you down.

4th–7th: Mild and quiet, until you discover that the kids have been busy finger-painting your white cat orange, "just like Garfield, Mommy!"

8th–12th: Pleasant, especially after your little one rediscovers her dollhouse, playing with it long enough for you not only to shower, but even to condition your hair—for the first time since the twentieth century.

13th–15th: Mostly fair, except for the part where your kids get to nap, one after the other, while you struggle to stay awake until dinnertime.

16th–19th: Unsettled, as the stomach flu rips through the house, starting with the baby and moving through the family to you—just in time for everyone else to relapse.

20th–21st: Hot, when your mom takes the kids for the weekend, giving you and Hubby much needed time alone without someone sleeping between you.

22nd: Changeable, because the child you call "Private Poopy Pants" will be very, very, uh, productive, during your niece's piano recital.

23rd–25th: Mixed, when somebody wants dessert but doesn't want to eat her carrots first, followed by clearing, when you realize there are carrots in the cake, anyhow.

26th–28th: Unseasonably mild, largely because Junior will be sucking up to you for that talking toy—the one with 236 pieces—that he wants for his birthday.

29th–31st: Tranquil, because everyone will finally be sleeping through the night, including you, the new puppy (what were you thinking?), and the offspring in the feety PJs next to you.

If You Think You're a "Cool Mom," Your Kids Think You're a Pushover

It was pathetic, really. My son and his playdate, both around five years old, were trying to out-burp each other, but all they could eke out were sad little burps that even an infant could emit after a couple of ounces of formula.

I know I was supposed to say, "Now, now, boys," and put an end to their poor manners, especially since the playdate's mother would most certainly not approve of their piggish behavior. I implored them to please stop, but they wouldn't listen. So, I found a better way to put an end to it.

"You call that a burp?" I asked. "*This* is a burp." I burped a deep, loud burp, the kind better described as a belch. The kind I had perfected with my big brother over cans of Coke decades earlier. Only this time, I did it without the aid of carbonation.

Yeah. I'm that good.

At first, both boys look stunned. Then they started to giggle. And giggle. And giggle, until my son's playdate collapsed to the ground in tears, gasping for air, as though this was the funniest thing he had ever witnessed in all of his five years. Funnier, even, than the Teletubbies and Cookie Monster combined. I mean, who'd ever seen a mom burp like a twelve-year-old boy who just chugged a liter bottle of Mountain Dew?

Uh oh, I thought. *What am I going to tell his mother?*

When she came to pick up her son, I told her the truth. Our boys would never again attempt to out-burp anyone because I'd completely shamed them with the biggest, loudest belch a mom has ever released for an audience, not counting Rosanne Barr's pre-game rendition of our national anthem, of course. I'd done her a favor, actually, and I'd earned a reputation as a "cool mom."

But there's a fine art to being a cool mom—an art that some moms don't quite fully understand. You can do cannonballs off the diving board, teach the kids how to lift a hockey puck over the goalie's legs, and, yes, belch like an extra in a Mike Meyers movie, but only if you temper it with good old-fashioned discipline—something this Mom-is-your-BFF generation sometimes has a hard time doing.

I may be the hostess of the frat house for fourth graders, but membership here has its privileges—privileges that I'll revoke the moment a kid crosses the line from light-hearted fun to bad behavior.

That's why the neighbor boy who enjoyed when I pitched baseballs to him in the driveway got sent home immediately when he wiped green slime on my cat. And the kid who loved running through the sprinkler I had set up was driven straight home when he wouldn't heed my rule, "Don't aim the Darth Vader sprinkler at my son's eyes again or you're outta here!"

In other words, I may be a cool mom, but I'm not my kids' friend, nor am I my kids' friends' friend, either. I'm still the boss.

The cool (but-I'm-still-the-boss) mom is the one whose house all the kids want to go to because it's loads of fun there. The cool (hey-wanna-try-a-wine-cooler?) mom is the one whose house all the kids want to go to because they can get away with a whole lot more than they can at home. What's the difference? See chart.

Cool-but-I'm-Still-the-Boss Mom	Cool-Hey-Wanna-Try-a-Wine-Cooler? Mom
Has a complete collection of Hilary Duff CDs at the ready in her minivan	Has a complete collection of Marilyn Manson CDs—and a T-shirt from his *Smells Like Children* concert tour
Can blow a bubble inside a bubble with a giant wad of gum, and is happy to show the kids how	Can blow a smoke ring inside another smoke ring, and is happy to show the kids how
Will take some sixth-grade girls to go see *High School Musical*, the story of two students who try out for their high school play	Will take some sixth-grade girls to go see *Rent*, the story of gay, bisexual, lesbian, and transgender artists and musicians struggling to survive in New York in the shadow of AIDS
Camped out to buy the latest Webkinz her ten-year-old son really wanted for his birthday	Camped out to buy the latest *Grand Theft Auto* game her ten-year-old son really wanted for his birthday
Coaches the softball team	Shouts, "That's alright, that's okay, you're gonna pump our gas someday!" at the opposing soft-ball team, a bunch of second graders whose jerseys are so big, they look like dresses

Will pull the kids behind her on a sled on the best hill in town	Will pull the kids behind her car on a sled in the best parking lot in town
Knows how to program the kids' phones to block out calls during school hours	Knows how to program the kids' phones to block out *The Sopranos* during school hours

MILF on board

In my neighborhood, there's a BMW that displays the bumper sticker, "It's all about me." Is it owned by a spoiled seventeen-year-old kid? No. Her mom. Life for women like her and their alpha-mom friends is indeed all about them and their Prada bags and Botox shots.

Strangely, it's also about how cool they are among their kids' friends. That explains the TV commercial featuring a mom who serves a snack to her fourteen-year-old son and his friend. When she leaves the room, the friend says, "Your mom is hot!" Overhearing what he said, she smirks as she pads away, presumably to go work on her abs some more.

I have three words for why it's just not cool for grown women to want to be considered hot by fourteen-year-old boys: Mary Kay Letourneau. Maybe it's hard to keep sight of that in a country where there's a *Hottest Mom in America* contest, not to mention a TV pilot called—and I'm not making this up—*MILF & Cookies.*

Sigh.

Even the *Today Show* ran "How to Be a Hot Mom," likely after the update on the Iraq War but before the "Lotsa Pasta!" cooking segment. I missed it all. I must have been busy scrubbing marker off my pants. So much for the hot mom contest.

I'm not saying that we should all wear muu-muus and let our hair go gray. There's nothing wrong with being "unapologetically sexy or simply dynamic women," even if it's the HotMomClub.com saying so. I'm all for ridding society of Mom jeans, and I've even been known to shop at The Gap (but that's mainly because I have the hips of a twelve-year-old boy and so do their women's pants).

But unless you're at a picnic for retired Playboy bunnies, it really isn't cool to wear a T-shirt bearing a word or two that, when Googled, brings up more porn than a computer with no spam filter. If you're truly a hot mom, everybody knows it already. You don't need to advertise it—especially at the junior high school.

Best Friends Forever! Please Take Our Poll

One holiday, my mom gave me a pillow embroidered with the words, "Always my daughter, now, too, my friend." I was thirty-three years old. Not thirteen. When I was a teen, I was most certainly not her friend, and not just because I may have told her "I hate you!" in a few moments of teen angst. No, because I was a teenager.

Some of today's mothers belong to the Susan Mayer School of Parenting. As with Teri Hatcher's *Desperate Housewives* character, kids aren't just kids, they're confidants, companions, and advisors. And it all starts with an opinion poll. . . .

I was at the mall one day when I witnessed a mother trying to get her child's opinion on something. "Do you want to leave, get something to eat, or do you want to go to the bookstore?" she asked her four-year-old in that cloying voice of desperation mothers use when they're about to completely lose control of their children to the allure of the rainbow sprinkles in the ice cream shop.

Clearly overloaded, the girl began spinning around in circles and ignoring her mother's opinion poll. "Now Olivia," Mom tried to rein in her daughter. "Do you want to get pizza, stop for a book. . . ." By now Olivia was spinning so fast she was getting dizzy and bumping into passers-by and their Macy's shopping bags. "Or would you like to. . . "

"Don't ask her. Tell her!" I barked, as Olivia spun herself to the ground like Veruca Salt down the garbage chute in Charlie and the Chocolate Factory. Her mom looked confused, as though I'd just given her directions to the food court in Punjabi. Clearly, nobody had ever suggested to her that she take charge and make decisions without first consulting her child.

I didn't stick around to see where Olivia chose to go, but I'm pretty sure that now that she's older, Olivia is the one in charge of everywhere they go, every day.

We're Going to Leave Right Now! Not.

If you let your four-year-old run your life, wait until you see how an older child can run it completely into the ground. Remember those empty threats you hurled at your preschooler? "If you don't behave now, we're going to leave the party!" Well, you never left the party. And your kid knows it.

Maybe you worried that you would look bad in front of the other parents if you scooped up your unruly child and went home. Maybe you'd feel bad he missed out on the birthday cake and goody bag full of mini chocolate bars and toy tattoos. Maybe you just didn't want to spend your weekend afternoon listening to him whine about how unfair it was that you left the party and how mean you are and how Jacob's mom would never do that. Maybe, but you got one peaceful Saturday afternoon in exchange for years of agony.

One fall day, I was waiting for a playdate to arrive. My son was looking forward to playing with his new pal from school, and I was anticipating letting them entertain each other so I could spend some time figuring out where the socks go in my house without having to stop and play the Game of Life between pairings.

Mom's Search-a-Word Puzzle

How often do you say these words? See if you can find them in the puzzle. They might be horizontal, vertical, or diagonal, backwards or forwards.

JUST A MINUTE

BECAUSE I SAID SO

NO

SAY THANK YOU

USE A NAPKIN

DON'T HIT YOUR SISTER

TURN THAT DOWN

YOU'RE GROUNDED

M	N	B	U	I	K	O	L	P	O	K	M	I	I	Y	T	I	L	O
D	O	N	T	H	I	T	Y	O	U	R	S	I	S	T	E	R	B	P
X	B	U	U	N	I	K	P	A	N	A	E	S	U	X	P	C	I	U
P	O	E	R	M	J	R	E	D	S	W	F	T	O	O	L	D	J	H
N	E	V	N	D	C	F	M	A	S	W	D	L	O	A	I	N	S	Z
O	K	Y	T	V	R	T	H	W	Q	U	E	R	M	N	M	I	K	I
M	S	R	H	E	T	U	N	I	M	A	T	S	U	J	Q	U	M	K
G	L	J	A	I	O	M	L	T	Y	H	U	C	H	R	E	I	L	P
F	A	X	T	P	Q	U	G	H	I	K	L	P	O	I	T	R	M	D
M	O	P	D	Y	O	U	R	E	G	R	O	U	N	D	E	D	L	Y
I	F	L	O	O	M	L	O	K	J	I	N	H	Y	B	T	V	B	K
V	W	B	W	V	B	G	R	T	H	J	U	O	E	C	X	Z	C	Y
H	Y	E	N	S	E	R	T	Y	U	O	P	K	B	H	K	D	I	M
S	O	S	D	I	A	S	I	E	S	U	A	C	E	B	P	M	E	E

Five minutes passed. Ten minutes passed. Fifteen minutes passed. He didn't show. So, I called his mom. "Oh yeah," she explained. "He's having such a good time playing down the street, I didn't want to interrupt him."

Oh, how I wanted to say, "Would the prince like his bath to be drawn after he has his lady fingers?" But I was speechless. She was afraid to ruin her son's fun by bringing him to a playdate—a playdate that my son would now miss out on because she didn't want to disturb her child's merriment.

I wondered how many birthday parties they've missed. I made sure I didn't touch their dog when I saw them out and about. After all, she might have decided that his annual rabies shots weren't important enough to interrupt his afternoon of chewing apart her shoes and pooping in the garden.

The kid whose parents failed to reel her in when she was all cute and curls and patent leather shoes later becomes the back-talking eye-roller who replaces the vodka she steals from their liquor cabinet with water. You know her: She's the kid who thinks shopping is a contact sport to be played every weekend at the mall with Mom's credit card. Or the boy who rides in the front seat long before he's legally allowed to and tunes out Mom's complaints with his iPod turned up way too loud. In other words, it's Olivia in Abercrombie and her brother in front of the Xbox. And they could be in your house, too, if you're not careful.

The Cool Mom State Line

The truly cool mom has one thing that the wannabes don't: boundaries. (Also, the ability to hang upside down from the monkey bars without falling out of her bra.) She knows where to draw the line, and how to keep the kids from crossing it.

She stays within boundaries . . .	She's gone too far . . .
She takes the kids for a spin on a gorgeous day with the top down on the convertible . . .	. . . and a whole lotta leg revealed, so that truckers honk at her as she races by while she waves appreciatively, as though they're complimenting her on her nice shoes.
She lets the kids stay up extra late during a sleepover at her house . . .	. . . so that they can watch her *Sex and the City* season one DVDs.
She asks the kids, "Do you want hot dogs or hamburgers . . ."	". . . or ribs or Mexican or chicken nuggets or . . ."
She sets up a jump for the kids to ride their bikes over . . .	. . . in the cul-de-sac of her street, half a block from her house—and her supervision.

If Forty Is the New Twenty, Why Are You Acting Like You're Twelve?

Does your husband have coolest-dad-on-the-block syndrome? If he's one of those parents who—get this—have installed snow-making equipment in their backyard so the kids always have somewhere to ski and sled, he may well be. The $800 snowblowers can make 180 cubic feet of fresh powder per hour, gobbling up to six gallons of water per minute. (I calculate it would take just one winter afternoon of snowy fun to drain our well, and $8,000 to dig it deeper.)

While you're outside grooming your mini ski trail, consider what you and Hubby are telling your kids: It's not enough for us to get you computers for your homework and the latest skateboarding gear because that's your passion. No, we need to buy the most outrageous, if not wasteful, gadgets so that everyone in the neighborhood knows we will stop at nothing to get you the best childhood money can buy. We are like Willie Wonka, here to make your stay with us the most amazing experience a kid could dream up.

We've gone mad over the latest and greatest stuff, and sometimes it makes us behave like teenagers. One pregnant woman camped outside a Chicago-area electronics store so she could buy the $500 PlayStation 3 when it first came out. It was just twelve degrees at night, and yet she camped out for three nights. Maybe *What to Expect When You're Expecting* should add a section called, "Preventing Frostbite for When You Camp Outside Circuit City." Our mothers didn't do such silly things, nor did they stand in line for hours so they could be among the first to buy the brand-new iPhone.

We've got to have the coolest gadgets and gizmos in the neighborhood. Why else would HGTV air entire shows dedicated to letting salespeople demonstrate the most outrageous kitchen gadgets? On *I Want That: Kitchens,* apparently what we want is tricked-out five-in-one refrigerators—with sections for both red and white wines—for $5,000. The five-in-one fridge or orthodontia for the kids? You choose.

But do we really need the hottest and most advanced digital video camera for a thousand bucks when we're still paying the hospital bills for the baby? And that $8,000 plasma screen TV of yours? I can see it from across the street. You should charge admission to help pay for it.

Jen's Tips for Being a Cool-but-Still-the-Boss Mom
Replace Your Filter

You've just spent the evening watching *Cops* on TV, and suddenly you wonder if your standards aren't a little too high. Once you've seen a guy get arrested for standing on the back of a pickup truck, waving his winkie at passers-by, you might start to think that you're as genteel as royalty. Why not let your guard down a bit and ease up on the kids? Because the winkie-waver shouldn't be your threshold for parenting, that's why.

Our parents had the *Happy Days'* Cunninghams and *The Cosby Show's* Huxtables as their fictional Mom and Dad role models. We have, what? Homer and Marge Simpson? Ozzie and Sharon "You're not going out because it's f^*#ing Christmas!" Osbourne?

With all this junk passing through nowadays, you really need to sift out a whole lot. Turn off the TV and put down your *Star* magazine and remind yourself that you are your children's filter at a time when there's never before been so much to protect them from. It's coming into the house through the TV, the computer, game consoles, cell phones, and their friends, whose parents might have big holes in their filters. And nine-year-olds just don't need to see winkie-wavers.

Use the TV and movie ratings as a guideline. Ask other mothers, who are a little more conservative in what they allow (and don't allow) their children to see, what they think. And quit cursing in front of the kids (and at Lowe's and in the school parking lot and while you're pumping gas . . .), would you?

Step back and look at your world as though you're showing around an American who's been living in the bush of Africa for the past thirty years. Then you'll realize what needs to be filtered from your home—and fast.

Don't Give It Away

You're really only a cool mom if the kids aren't expecting the cool stuff all the time. Think of yourself as Bruce Springsteen at the Stone Pony. Every now and then, rumors circulate that the rock star might make an unscheduled appearance at the Jersey Shore club where he got his start. Sometimes Bruce shows. Sometimes he doesn't. The fact that he doesn't always show makes it all that more special when he does.

Similarly, if rumors are swirling around your minivan that you might treat the kids and their friends to ice cream today, don't promise a thing. Let them speculate, and then sometimes, don't deliver. Like Bruce, it's all so much sweeter when you least expect it.

If you're the mom who always serves homemade chocolate chip cookies when the kids are over to play, they'll come to expect it, like strawberries and cream at Wimbledon. Then you become not so much a cool mom as a waitress for unruly patrons.

The cool mom isn't always fun, fun, fun! Sometimes, she's cranky because taxes are due or she left the milk in the hot car for three hours. The kids—and their friends—need to know that you have grown-up concerns (and therefore, grown-up moods). So when the cool mom comes out to play, it's more like the season

Mom's Word Scramble

Unscramble the words to find the answers:

1. Causing trouble or anxiety; worrisome

   E H T L F Y I A M U Y G

2. Extremely annoying or displeasing

   L Y E R E L O

3. To behave in an inappropriate way

   R T W I T W N S F L H T E E I

4. Not in keeping with what is correct or proper

   S R T B L Y O E H I E L V R 4 0

5. Playful in an appropriate way

   O M O O C M L

Answers: 1. THE FAMILY GUY, 2. EYEROLL, 3. FLIRT WITH TWEENS,
4. BELLY SHIRT OVER 40, 5. COOL MOM

premiere of *The Suite Life of Zach and Cody* than a rerun. It's something you don't see everyday.

Because I'm the Mommy, That's Why

Every time you feel the urge to be your child's best friend, play house. And you be the Mommy, okay? Not the big sister. Not the new kid who just moved in next door. The Mom.

The Mom can and will play Candy Land or Office or Super Mario Brothers. But the Mom has to quit at some point to make dinner. And she won't tolerate cheating or whining. And she certainly doesn't shout, "In your face, Chloe!" when she gets the Princess Frostine card.

The Mom will take a bunch of tweens to the mall, but she won't try on the "Sex without love is just exercise" T-shirt at Abercrombie and Fitch. She'll take the kids down the Rocket Raft water slide at the amusement park, but she knows enough to stay off the snowboarding trails during Friday Night's Teen Throwdown. Why? Because she's the mommy, that's why.

Maybe it's true that today's kids are more savvy than we were, but that's probably because they're exposed to a lot more than we were and at much younger ages. Just because Aeropostale, MTV, and Lindsay Lohan say ten is the new fifteen, doesn't mean that your kids are mature enough to be your best pal. So save the diatribe about how your "stupid sister" has gone and done it again—falling in love with the wrong guy and spending all her money on a tummy tuck—for someone your own age.

Acting Your Age	**Acting Like, You Know, a Teenager**
Your cell phone ring sounds like a phone ringing.	Your cell phone ring plays *Party Like a Rock Star*—right in the middle of the sermon at church.
You walk around with that Bluetooth thingy stuck in your ear when you're supervising a major event where you're in charge of dozens of people.	You walk around with that Bluetooth thingy stuck in your ear at Thanksgiving dinner where you're in charge of the salad.
Your email address has your kids' names in it.	Your email address is "toosexy-formystroller."
You text your accountant to ask a quick question about tax write-offs.	You text your accountant to ask a quick question about tax write-offs—when he's at the other end of the table.
You check MySpace to see what your teen is up to.	You check MySpace to see how many "friends" you've made since you put up your page.

SECRET FOURTEEN

Don't Share Your Kid's Quality Time with Your BlackBerry

Do they make safety straps for BlackBerries on roller coasters? Because they should. It certainly would have come in handy for the father I saw at the Jersey Shore, sitting next to his daughter on the Himalaya thrill ride, talking on his cell phone. One good twist and turn the wrong way, and that BlackBerry was going mobile in an entirely new way.

The ride spun around. The daughter squealed with delight. The father orchestrated a business deal with colleagues half a world away. Or maybe he was making reservations at Applebee's. I dunno. But I do know that he couldn't be completely *there* for his kid, even though he was there in the seat next to her, spinning and talking. Talking and spinning.

But then there's a whole lot of that going on these days.

I could make a sweeping generalization that technology is taking a megabyte out of the modern parent–child relationship, but I'm not sure that it really is. That dad's BlackBerry probably made it possible for him to be at the beach in the first place, rather than in his office while his daughter colored in the corner, waiting for him to finish making his deal.

I confess that I have been interviewed by reporters on my cell phone while walking through the cereal aisle at the supermarket, pointing to boxes of Cheerios, and then at my son, and then at the shopping cart, all while trying to sound clever and quotable. Cell phones make it possible for today's parents to blend work with family in a way that our parents never could.

But they also make us act like asses sometimes.

Work Never Ends

My grandfather, who ran his own successful real estate development business, left the office every afternoon at five and rarely answered work calls at home. When someone called at two a.m. to tell him that the wall of one of his buildings had fallen on some cars, he rolled over and went back to sleep. "What am I going to do about it at two a.m.?" he later explained.

Nowadays, though, you'd better be available at two a.m. And when you're on the Himalaya ride. And next to the sale on Cocoa Puffs. Unless you're going on a month-long visit to Antarctica, people expect to be able to reach you whenever and wherever. Heck, there's even wifi in the hospital, where I wrote portions of this book. I text messaged my lawyer at four a.m. (nobody sleeps in the hospital)—and he *answered*. He was up with the baby anyway, he explained.

All this connectedness has been great for home-based businesses like mine. Nowadays it's okay if your client can hear little Johnny ask you to open the Play-Doh while you're on the phone with him, because, chances are, he's ordering some juice for his kid at Starbucks at the same time.

But if we don't draw a line somewhere between the personal and the professional, what will we get? BlackBerry orphans.

Our kids are the first generation of such a group, children of "furtive thumb typers" as the *Wall Street Journal* tagged them, who just can't put down their personal digital assistants and go eat dinner with the rest of the family. The *Wall Street Journal* ran a feature on parents who are so addicted to their BlackBerries that their kids are taking intervention-like steps to get them to stop. One kid even banned his mother's use of her PDA at the dinner table. So what did she do? She hid it in the bathroom and developed a weak bladder.

My architect once said, "When you work from home, you're never fully at work, and you're never fully at home." I think that's also true of any job that has your cell phone number or hands out PDAs to employees. Just a few years ago, I wouldn't hear back from editors or reporters when I emailed them during my mom-induced working hours of eight to midnight. Now, though, they answer right away, probably while they're watching *American Idol* or tucking in the kids. I can wait, folks. Really. And so can you.

As more of us walk around with Internet access, we expect responses faster and faster. And we expect responses whether we're taking a vacation day or just running errands around town. In the office? That's nice. But it doesn't really matter anymore. Just ask the kids.

Masters of Nothing

My mother-in-law has a cell phone, but she rarely turns it on. Why? Because then she'd have to pull her car over to answer it, and that's too much trouble. So, when she's taking the 50-mile trip to our house, we have no way of reaching her to suggest she take a different route because there's an accident followed by 12 miles of traffic along her route. After all, we wouldn't want her to have to pull over to chat.

But if one of her offspring or their spouses were en route, we'd not only be able to call with the warning, but also recommend an alternate route via GPS. The driver could also check for highly rated Chinese restaurants along the way to pick up dinner, find out the movie times for that evening and read about Lindsay

Lohan's latest arrest. Oh, and find out the weather for Saturday, too. And search for a sale on bath towels, and see if the latest Magic Treehouse book is on sale yet and . . .

We can do more things at once than our parents ever could and yet they're the generation who invented the three-martini lunch. Go figure. But then, how did parents have their time sucked away back before the Internet, Xbox, and CNBC? We can read the news crawl *and* pay attention to what the anchors are saying at the same time. Also, program the TiVo. When did we learn to do all that?

Maybe that's why we think we can simultaneously read *Goodnight Moon* and text message our accountants about writing off the corner of the living room where the laptop port sits. Or cheer our kids on the basketball court and check our stocks at the same time. Or host a conference call during a playdate. And maybe we can. But should we? Not all the time, no. It's not fair to the kids.

Children know when you're not really paying attention to them. When my husband recently told our son it would take him two more minutes to finish talking to the neighbor (about gutters—yawn), my son mumbled, "Oh great. Two more minutes means ten minutes at least!" And he was right. There was another ten minutes all about gutters still in him, during which he didn't notice that the boys were retrieving wiffle balls from (aka trampling) the pachysandra.

When our faces are glued to a computer screen or our fingers are madly typing on a PDA, we're paying as much attention to our kids as they're paying to us when they sit slack-jawed in front of the PlayStation, making empty promises about cleaning up the mess in their rooms. And they know it.

I can't imagine my father hovering over the newly invented answering machine thirty years ago, anxious to reply to whatever pressing work matter arose. So what are today's CrackBerry addicts so hooked on? Sports scores, weather reports, celebrity news, and spam, all at your fingertips, 24/7.

Wired on Wireless

Are You Addicted to Your Gadgets and Gizmos?
A Questionnaire

How often do you check your email during your free time?
    a. Every few days
    b. Every few hours
    c. Once an hour
    d. Hold on a sec. I just have to answer this email. Oh! And that one, too.

Do you hide your BlackBerry from your family?
    a. Never
    b. Sometimes
    c. You didn't look in the plant in the living room, did you?

Have you ever missed a family function because you're too busy with your PDA?
    a. No
    b. Once or twice
    c. cant write kids watching

Do you find normal face-to-face interactions difficult?
    a. Never.
    b. Sometimes.
    c. LOL! nvr. Not found 404. ;-)

Do you experience pain in your thumb?
  a. Never
  b. Rarely
  c. Every Friday, but I rest it all weekend.
  d. ow

How often have you had difficulty remembering the night before because of your addiction?
  a. Never
  b. Just that time in Vegas after the big convention, but I swear I'll never do that again!
  c. Uh. Lemme check my Internet history and my Sent Items. What did you want to know?

Has a friend, relative, or doctor suggested you cut down?
  a. No
  b. Yes, but I emailed her and now we're friends again
  c. Well, I took him off my Contacts database and out of my Five.

Have you ever felt guilty after using your PDA?
  a. No, not really.
  b. Almost, but then I noticed the teacher kept hers in her lap during our parent-teacher conference, too.
  c. Only that time my sister found me with it in the ladies' room at her wedding. Twice.
  d. Who gave you my BlackBerry Addict chat room name?

The Computer's Down

What I remember most about Monday nights in my freshman dorm is the orchestra of typewriters. Everyone on my Communications-major floor had twelve-page papers due on

Tuesday, so we'd type away at our IBM Selectrics through the night. Except Stephanie. My friend Stephanie had one of the very first PC Jr.'s, so we'd never hear "Uuuuuuuuuuuugh! I've got to type it all over again!" coming from her room. Rather, we'd slip her money so we could use her computer.

We were the first generation to benefit from the technology boom at a relatively young age. And though we've never sat in our rooms at night texting our friends about what happened in algebra class, we like what technology can do to make our lives easier. That's why when we lose our cell phones, we're lost, too. And when the computer goes down. And when TiVo gets all messed up, recording *American Graffiti* instead of the season finale of *American Idol*. (Drat! Is it online? Oh no! The computer's down!)

We all remember calling home from the school nurse's office only to listen to ring after ring after unanswered ring, because Mom wasn't home and we didn't own an answering machine yet. We don't want to go back to those dark days.

But we need to remember that before our BlackBerries, laptops, GPS systems, TiVos, Bluetooths, and wifi, we all survived just fine. We had electricity. We had heat. We had *Dallas*.

Now, we have our kids. And we should pay more attention to them before they get their own BlackBerries, laptops, GPS systems, TiVos, Bluetooths, and wifi and don't have time for us anymore.

Jen's Tips for Stopping Way Short of Taking Technology Too Far
Bring Back the Busy Signal

When voice mail first became popular, my cousin (the one still holding fireworks while the cops drove up) wanted none of it. His reason: "Now I've got to call all those people back." When callers got busy signals instead of voice mail, the onus was on them to call back. Voice mail, my cousin reasoned, meant more work for him. And he was right.

In an era when we're expected to be reachable all the time, perhaps we should have our own proverbial busy signals more often. If we were just a little less accessible to people from work, the kids' school, and the neighborhood, maybe we'd be a little more accessible to our kids.

Do you really need to check your email before you go to bed? Can the friend who's calling just as you're putting dinner on the table wait until later, perhaps tomorrow? Will your boss really think you're slacking off if you don't answer your phone while you're boarding the commuter train? That's why voice mail was invented. Just ask my cousin.

Conventional wisdom once estimated that technology would let us all get our work done so quickly, we'd have three-day weekends every week. Instead, it's lengthened our workdays and weeks so that we're answering business calls during our weekend Home Depot trips and baby showers.

And while it affords us opportunities to be on the sidelines at our kids' games instead of at the office, late once again, we can take it a little too far. Like on the Himalaya at the Jersey Shore, for example. Don't answer your emails so quickly or everyone will come to expect it. When you're at your daughter's softball game, say you're "tied up in a meeting." Don't be so quick to volunteer your help, time, and resources. Be a little more inaccessible, so you can be more accessible to your kids.

Use Technology for Good, Not Evil

I'm writing this on my laptop in the waiting area at my sons' dentist's office so that later we can hang out at the lake together. I won't bring my laptop to the lake, and not just because I don't want to get sand between the keys. Because I've carved out that time to be with my kids.

I've managed to build a home-based (and sometimes, dentist's office-based) business around my kids' schedules, but it takes a lot of orchestrating and rearranging. Without technology, though, I couldn't do this at all. Yet I'm very careful not to cross over to the dark side.

It'd be easy to fill the hours between the end of school and dinnertime with work, but I rarely do. I just don't want my kids' after-school memories to be of the back of my head in front of a computer screen while I shush them. I'd much rather spend that time handing out ice pops to a posse of sweaty, filthy boys who are playing soccer in my backyard. I am the hostess of the frat house for fourth graders, after all.

I do, however feel the pull of my email when I'm not at my computer, or when my PDA is buried in my purse while I'm out. The Internet never closes. But if I made myself available all the time to everybody who visits my website from every time zone, not to mention all those moms who drop by my site between night feedings, I'd never sleep.

Instead, I use technology for good in these ways:

No one can hear you scream on email. I didn't talk to editors on the phone much when my kids were little. Rather, I used email as much as possible because it allowed me to contact them even though I could hear a cranky kid waking up from a nap. Plus, I could email at odd hours when they weren't in their offices but I was at my desk. You can start and stop an email message numerous times to put wheels back on Tonka trucks, break up fights, and play Candy Land, and no one would ever know it. Plus, no one can hear you lose your cool with your kids on email. *Slipping over to the evil side: When you pay more attention to what's in your email box than who's at your dinner table.*

You can look like you're working when you're not. All it takes is one quick email that says, "Thanks for sending this contract. I will review it and get back to you tomorrow." And then you can go back to watching your kid get her white belt in karate class. *Slipping over to the evil side: Actually reviewing the contract during class and sending your black-line comments back. If you follow up with a phone call and your kid sees you do it, you might as well play* The Evil Empire *song in the background, Darth.*

Make the most of waiting time. While all the other moms are reading magazines or cleaning out their cars as they wait for the school bus to return from the class trip, you can catch up with work on your laptop. The same goes for the kids' dentist office, the hair salon/barber shop, the preschool pick-up line, and those incredibly long indoor swim meets where your kid is in the water all of five minutes for the day. *Slipping over to the evil side: Bringing your laptop to piano or dance recitals, where your tap-tap-tapping annoys the other parents who are trying to watch their kids.*

The Search for Parenting Information, Then and Now

Then	Now
Find a rash on the baby.	Find a rash on the baby.
↓	↓
Ask your mother for her opinion on it.	Ask your mother for her opinion on it.
↓	↓
Take the baby to her pediatrician, who says it's heat rash and prescribes an ointment to treat it.	Google "rash."
↓	↓
Rash goes away.	Visit a medical website that outlines numerous rashes along with some rather disgusting accompanying photos.
	↓

Worry that it could be either eczema, heat rash, or granuloma annulare, which—oh my God!—may be associated with diabetes or thyroid disease.

↓

Google "thyroid disease."

↓

Discover that hypothyroidism in children can decrease their growth rate and cause lethargy.

↓

Panic, because the baby was "only" in the 75th percentile for height at her last check-up, but in the 80th percentile at the check-up before.

↓

Wonder if she's been napping too much lately.

↓

Email your mother to ask her if anyone in the family had thyroid problems and to ask how long the baby napped today at her house.

↓

Spend half an hour reading heart-wrenching thyroid message boards.

Mom emails back to report that Aunt Mary had hypothyroidism when she was eighty-two, and the baby napped *three hours*!

↓

Visit a website where people who represent themselves with cartoon drawings and nicknames like "Petunia89" all agree that it's genetic (except one guy with no cartoon who calls himself "Yoda69," and really, who can trust him?)

↓

Spend hours frantically researching thyroid problems and diabetes.

↓

Take the baby to her pediatrician, who says it's heat rash and prescribes an ointment to treat it.

↓

Rash goes away.

CONCLUSION

What I've Learned by Mothering from the Middle

My minivan looks (and smells) a lot like my aunt's Country Squire station wagon did thirty years ago. Various balls and rolled-up dirty socks tumble around when I make turns, and all sorts of things have flown forward at stoplights, including (but certainly not limited to) half-used *Mad-Libs* pads, sweaty, stinky shin guards, and a rubber Spider-Man glove programmed to sound like it's making webs, any size. And yet, I'm not really a Slacker Mom. After all, I can recite my kids' schedules for the next week without using a calendar as a teleprompter.

Still, I'm not much of a Super Mom, either, even though I sure have tried to be. Unlike my mother's organized station wagon from back in the day, my car has just two maps: one for the county I lived in thirteen years ago and one for Martha's Vineyard, even though we haven't vacationed there since 2002. Now and then, I can find Purell, Band-Aids, spare change, *and* a pen that works in my minivan, but I'm hardly a reliable supplier.

In short, I mom from the middle. And it's been good for both me and my kids. It took me years to find this safe, happy place between Super Mom and Slacker Mom, largely because I didn't even start looking for it until I was well into motherhood. For a long time, I didn't even know it was there.

Like many twenty-first-century moms, I thought I was supposed to strive for perfection. I spent a lot of time researching educational toys, creating teachable moments, and honing my kids' fine motor skills, all the while worrying that I wasn't doing enough for my children.

But trying to keep up with the Super Moms and their high standards proved too exhausting and overwhelming for me. When my husband's family arranged a week-long trip to the Jersey Shore the summer my older son was six, I stayed home. I was so burnt out from filling a hundred hours a week with educational yet entertaining activities for my children, I figured I'd get more of a vacation home alone watching chick flicks on TV than I would at the beach with my family, surrounded by free help. All by myself, I didn't have to be perfect.

And yet, I sometimes slipped into the abyss of slacker mothering, wondering if I really needed to be quite so diligent about what my kids saw on TV or wore on their backs when so many other parents weren't. Slacking off seemed so much easier than making all those lesson plans for my teachable moments. I even started to aspire to be like the celebrity moms I saw on the cover of *People,* oblivious to the fact that I could never be like them without a staff—and a large movie deal to pay for such a staff.

But as my kids got older, I started seeing the consequences of what the Slacker Moms were doing to their kids, who were cursing at and punching other kids on the soccer teams I coached and quoting *Borat* on the third-grade class trip. Certainly this wasn't the time to ease up on monitoring what my kids watched, read, and spewed out at home or on their school bus, where fifth graders were showing R-rated movies on their parent-supplied portable gadgets.

Keeping up with Super Mom was no good for me. But sinking into Slacker Mom territory was no good for my kids. The spot in the middle, however, has proven to be just right for me and my family. Here, I can ease up on the super-grueling super-parenting and enjoy my kids—and being a mother. Here, I can make sure my kids aren't tainted by the raunchy media culture that's trapping our kids at younger ages. Here, I can be a good mom while turning out perfectly fine kids. And you can, too.

Remember these fourteen secrets the next time you contemplate signing up your three-year-old for a ("Let's all sit now!") music class when he'd much rather be outside playing on the slide. Or when you're thinking of sending your tween to school in a "Certified Diva" T-shirt.

But remember this most of all: You're a good mom. You really are.

Parenting Now	Parenting Then
Baby Einstein	Big Bird
Fine motor skills evaluation	Crayons and paper. Have fun!
Kindergarten readiness tests with placement and/or tutoring suggestions	Birth certificate that proves your kid is five years old
Traveling soccer try-outs	Recreation soccer meeting: "You take these thirteen, and I'll take thirteen, and Joe will take the last thirteen."

Personal baseball coaches with one-on-one drills once a week	Dad in the backyard with his old mitt
Camping out for dance recital tickets three months ahead of time, after spending $150 on your daughter's dance costume	"Be there Saturday at two. Wear your tutu."
Birthday party with limo to pick up kids to take them to a recording studio, where they'll record their own personal DVDs, followed by dinner at The Rainbow Room	Pizza, cake, and games in the backyard. The kitchen, if it rains.
Xbox, TiVo, Netflix, HBO, IM, and a cell phone	A dime for the pay phone and "Pong" hooked up to the TV
Sweet Sixteen party with two hundred guests, a $1,000 dress, a band, and, did you order a shrimp buffet and a chocolate fountain? Wow! (What will you do for her wedding?)	Took all the girls to go see *Sixteen Candles,* starring Molly Ringwald, followed by ice cream at Friendly's.
SAT tutoring and college application consultants	An IBM Selectric typewriter and a bottle of Wite-Out
Kids move home—with spouse and children—until they save enough money to buy a house	"Bye, kids! Be sure to write!"

Acknowledgments

There are a lot of people who helped make it possible for me to write this book. Here's my chance to say thank you. To my editor, Shana Drehs, who brought out the best of my words and made them shine. To all the folks at Sourcebooks for all their hard work and dedication. To my agent, Wendy Sherman, for finding a nice home for my book. To Ed Albowicz, manager and friend. And to Robin Blakely, my right-hand woman and more like a sister than you'll ever know.

To my oncologist, Dr. Julian Decter, my radiation oncologist, Dr. Alison Grann, and all the staff at New York Hospital who helped make me healthy again. To the Smalleys, Tchikatilovs, and LoCascios for your food and friendship, and for caring for my kids like your own. To the entire Kinnelon community for helping us when we needed it most.

To Monica Singer, Jenna Schnuer, Gwen Moran, Danielle Marcantuono, Diane and Pete Loughlin, Marybeth Hicks, Carolyn Bodden, Cherry Key, Ashley Formento, Rachel Weingarten, the "Ladies," BUGS, FLX, my MommaSaid columnists, the Wacky Wig contestants, and the BHG crew for helping me through a rough time with your hospital visits, care packages, and friendship.

To my parents, my brother, my in-laws, my cousins, and my aunt and uncle for pitching in and for standing by me. (I'll never forget the day my brother showed up in my hospital room with my iPod filled with songs he'd downloaded for me. Thank you.)

To my husband, Pete, to whom this book is dedicated. I never knew how much I truly love you until now. I am, indeed, a lucky woman.

And to Nicholas and Christopher, who continue to be the light of my life, even when you're tracking mud across our new kitchen floor.

About the Author

America's top parenting humorist Jen Singer is the creator of MommaSaid.net, a Forbes Best of the Web online community for moms who need comic relief and a pat on the back. The founder of "*Please* Take My Children to Work Day," Jen writes the Good Grief! blog about parenting tweens for GoodHousekeeping.com. A Swiffer Amazing Woman of the Year, Jen and her humor have appeared in the *New York Times, Parenting, First for Women,* and many more. She lives in northern New Jersey with her husband, their two sons, and a saxophone that squeaks.

A Note from the Author

I had four chapters of this book left to write when I found out I had cancer. One day I was finishing up my manuscript while juggling the final weeks of the school year, and the next I was enduring a painful bone marrow biopsy to determine if cancer had spread throughout my body. Soon, I'd learn the lessons of my own book the hard way: I had to completely let go without going too far. My health—and my kids—were counting on it.

After my doctor diagnosed my non-Hodgkin's lymphoma, my publisher gave me a six-week deadline extension, and my brother gave me his laptop. Some days, I cranked out pages at a time in my hospital bed while chemotherapy drugs infused through tubes attached to my body. Other days, I could barely write a sentence before falling asleep for hours.

Yet somehow, I managed to maintain my sense of humor. In fact, even I can't tell which chapters I wrote B.C.—before cancer—and which I wrote afterwards. Writing kept my spirits up, and, perhaps, my white blood cell counts.

But it wasn't easy. I spent the last few weeks of my kids' school year in the hospital. Every night, my boys played the piano for me over the phone while I fought back tears. I missed their Cub

Scouts moving up ceremony, the second-grade class party and the last day of school. Most of all, I missed my kids.

By the time I turned in my manuscript in August, I'd finished half of my chemotherapy treatments. The tumor in my lung, which had been the size of a softball, had shrunk to the size of a walnut. I was tired, weak, and bald, but my kids didn't care as long as I was home, which, by the way, was under construction. In fact, I edited parts of this book while sawdust fell on my head from upstairs and strange men hammered and sawed on the other side of the wall.

When a friend dropped by after our kitchen was gutted and our siding was removed, she said, "If this house isn't a metaphor for what's going on with you, I don't know what is." And here I thought I looked better than that. I mean, I was bald, but the house was naked.

We were very fortunate to have so much help. Every week, my friend Susan organized neighbors who cooked for us. Every Sunday, my friend Kim sent me a calendar which listed the neighbors who'd drive my kids to swim team practice, pick them up at science camp, or take them home for a playdate. Both sets of grandparents, my sister-in-law, and my husband (aka King of the Laundry) picked up the slack. Meanwhile, I snoozed on the couch. (You know, between all that hammering and sawing.)

I could have shut my bedroom door and hidden all summer, but I didn't because I was frightened of what might happen. I had a vision of my kids, all grown-up, remembering when their mother had cancer as "the summer I took up smoking" or "the year I took to blowing up ant holes with M-80s," or worse. Though I couldn't be there for my boys the way I normally was, I knew I still had to be there, even if that simply meant playing charades and giggling for half an hour.

Other people might find solace in the likes of Maya Angelou or Hallmark. I turned to Stephen Colbert, who said, "You can't laugh and be afraid at the same time." So, I set up a Wacky Wig Contest, designed to let friends make me look as ridiculous as possible in my time of need.

Every week, all kinds of crazy wigs appeared in our mail. The kids ran around the house in the Marge Simpson, the Achy Breaky Heart and the Heatmeiser. I modeled them and posted the photos on MommaSaid.net for voting. Together, we laughed in the face of cancer. And you know what? The kids turned out okay.

I've finished my chemotherapy and radiation treatments, and my hair has grown back enough that I look like I'm either a marine home from Iraq or a back-up singer for Annie Lennox. Shortly after New Year's Day, my oncologist called me with spectacular news: I am in remission. What's more, our construction is done, and the house looks beautiful. It seems I've made it through the hardest part. At least, I sure do hope so.

I learned a lot of things because of cancer. I learned a lot while writing this book. Most of all, I learned that I am a good mom—and that my kids aren't so bad either.

Jen Singer
February, 2008